ROSE ELLIOT'S
VEGETARIAN
CHRISTMAS

ROSE ELLIOT'S
VEGETARIAN CHRISTMAS

Over 150 Recipes for Every Festive Occasion

HarperCollins*Publishers*

ACKNOWLEDGEMENTS

In keeping with its theme, working on this book was a particularly happy experience – the Christmas spirit seemed to predominate at every stage, and I'd like to express my warmest thanks to everyone who took part and helped to create the book. Firstly, Sarah Sutton, of Thorsons, for suggesting the idea; and Robin Wood, Polly Powell and Barbara Dixon, of Collins, for taking it up so enthusiastically; my agent, Barbara Levy, for arranging the contract and for all her usual support and good advice. I'd like to say a special 'thank you' to Isabel Moore for being such a pleasure to work with and organizing the project so well, including assembling such an excellent team: Martin Brigdale, who took the beautiful photographs; Lyn Rutherfood, who prepared the food so splendidly, and Marion Price, who collected the tableware and decorations which set it off at its best, and the artistic director, Kelly Flynn who turned it all into such a good-looking book. Finally, I'd like to thank all the members of my family, who, from my childhood onwards, have made Christmas such a wonderful and special time.

First published in 1992 by
HarperCollins Publishers London
Reprinted 1992

Created exclusively for HarperCollins by Isabel Moore

Text © Rose Elliot 1992
Photographs © Martin Brigdale 1992
All rights reserved

The Author asserts the moral right to be identified as
the author of this work

Designer: Kelly Flynn
Photographer: Martin Brigdale
Illustrations: Claire Davies

For HarperCollins Publishers
Commissioning Editor: Polly Powell
Project Editor: Barbara Dixon

A CIP catalogue record for this book is available
from the British Library

ISBN 0 00 412681 5

Typeset in Palatino by Servis Filmsetting, Manchester
Colour reproductions by NM Reproductions, Nr Bath
Printed and bound in Italy by Amilcare Pizzi, S.p.A.

CONTENTS

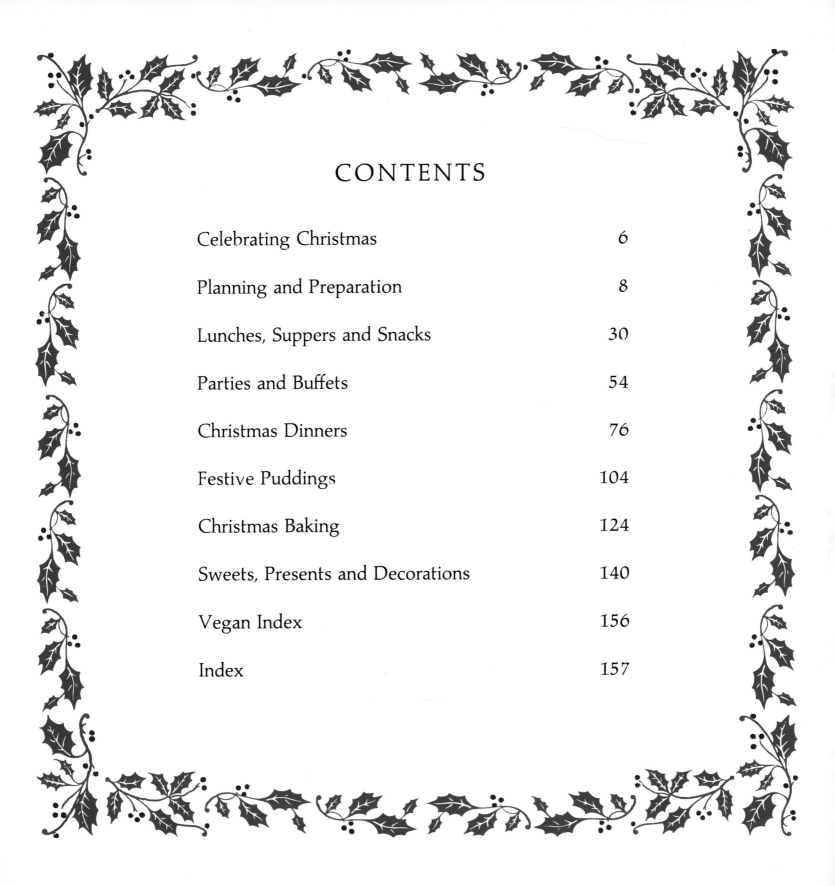

CELEBRATING CHRISTMAS

I love Christmas. The fun, the memories, the spicy smells, the goodwill. Yes, like everyone else I deplore the exploitation and the pressures, the Christmas catalogues dropping through the letter box before the end of the summer and the carols being played in shops in November, but however much I may grumble about these things, the Christmas magic always gets to me in the end.

We always had especially wonderful Christmases when I was a child. My parents, sister and I, along with my aunt, uncle and cousins, always spent Christmas with my grandparents in their house in the country. This was great fun, with lots of excitement and racing around the house and garden, as well as singing – and listening to – carols, a beautiful service on Christmas Eve in the chapel there, and a short meditation at noon on Christmas Day. Then we had Christmas dinner, and opened all the presents which were kept under the tree until after the Queen's speech.

What really made Christmas special, though, was my grandmother's approach to it. My grandmother, Grace Cooke, was a very remarkable woman, a mystic and seer. Although she considered herself to be a Christian, and had a deep love and respect for Jesus, she thought of Christmas as being symbolic of an older, universal truth, not confined to the Christian church. She saw the birth of the baby Jesus in a dark cave or in a stable, as a symbol of the awakening of the light of love in every human heart.

It was her belief (and mine, too) that all of us have that light of love – the spark of divinity – within ourselves. We express it when we give and receive love, and it is at these times we feel happy within ourselves; but when we cut ourselves off from that centre, we become out of sorts with ourselves and others. We are probably most aware of this power when we fall in love – our heart really opens, and everything seems magical. We also notice it at Christmas, when we think about other people more than we usually do and there is a general feeling of goodwill and the dropping of barriers.

The sense of universality and brotherhood which this approach to Christmas gives, appeals to me very much: no race or religious creed is excluded; the awakening of the light of love in our hearts is something which we can all experience and celebrate. For me it is especially significant that Christmas is at the time of the winter solstice when, in the northern hemisphere, the sun – or light – begins to get closer to us again.

All are reasons for celebration, of which preparing and eating wonderful meals together is a natural and important part. Christmas cooking is, for most people, the great culinary feast, not to say feat, of the year. Even people who do not do a great deal of cooking during the rest of the year find themselves doing so at Christmas and need good, reliable recipes. This is especially true if they find themselves having to cook for one or more of the increasing number of vegetarians!

This book aims to answer this need. It's a collection of all the tips, ideas and best recipes that I've gathered over the years, as well as exciting new ones. So whether you've just one vegetarian to cater for, or a crowd, or just want some fresh and delicious ideas for festive food, I hope you'll find it helpful: a warm and practical cook's companion.

Happy Christmas!

Rose Elliot

PLANNING AND PREPARATION

One of the great pleasures of traditional Christmas cooking is that not only can it be done well in advance, but it's actually all the better for it. So when new supplies of plump dried fruit fill the shops, you can fill the house with the warm and spicy smells of Christmas and get the cake, pudding and mincemeat made and stored away, knowing that they will only improve with time. Shopping for ingredients and equipment, and the making of these delicious, traditional dishes, can be fitted in over several days and weeks, giving you a chance to produce them when it is convenient for you.

Good Christmas planning can begin as early as October, with the listing and buying of ingredients, the checking of tins and equipment, the making of menu plans and the gradual filling up of the storecupboard and freezer. Done in this relaxed and gradual way, Christmas preparations can be enjoyed as the pleasure they really are. One of the bonuses is that there is time for other people, especially the children, to join in if they wish, which adds to the fun and sense of anticipation. Then, when Christmas arrives, with the majority of the work done, you can relax (mostly!) with everyone else, and have a really good time. I have found that the earlier I make my preparations, the more I enjoy them – and the more I enjoy Christmas itself.

Having said that, I must add that I know that Octobers don't always work out like that, nor Novembers, and there have certainly been times when I have been making a Christmas cake in the week before Christmas and icing it on Christmas Eve! So in this book you'll find a wonderful Last-

Minute Christmas Cake, as well as plenty of not-too-demanding but rather special recipes for every meal, since I know that even people who don't cook or entertain a great deal during the year find that they do so at Christmas, either through desire or necessity. I hope you'll enjoy them.

I've also considered the fact that many people are, I know, cooking for one or more vegetarians as well as for meat-eaters. Under these circumstances, there are two courses of action: sometimes everyone can enjoy a completely vegetarian meal; at other times, you can share the vegetables and accompaniments (as long as these are made without animal products like meat stock, gelatine or dripping etc), and the vegetarians can have their own main course.

Often, in practice, I've found that the meat-eaters like to share this, too, as a kind of extra side-dish to their meat, so you need to make enough. I rather like it when this happens; I certainly like to avoid a 'them' and 'us' approach, more a mutual acceptance of dietary preferences and a sharing of food. Of course, this does inevitably mean extra work for the cook, which is where advance preparation is such a help.

Most of the main courses in this book freeze really well, as do parts of the meal, such as crêpes, sauces, stuffings, pastry cases and so on, so that if you have some of these stashed away in the freezer, you can combine them with fresh vegetables, eggs, milk or cheese (if they eat these) and put together a delicious dish for one or two unexpected vegetarians in no time at all.

You'll find my specific freezer recommendations and standby recipes later in this chapter. But to begin the preparations, and get yourself into the mood early, I recommend that you stick with tradition and make the cake, the pudding and the pies first.

TRADITIONAL CHRISTMAS CAKE

700 g/1½ lb mixed dried
fruit
100 g/4 oz candied peel,
chopped
225 g/8 oz glacé cherries
150 ml/5 fl oz sherry or
orange juice
250 g/9 oz plain
wholewheat flour and
plain white flour, mixed
1 tsp baking powder
½ tsp mixed spice
¼ tsp freshly grated
nutmeg
250 g/9 oz butter or soft
vegetarian margarine
250 g/9 oz soft brown
sugar
4 eggs, lightly beaten
grated rind of 1 orange
grated rind of 1 lemon
50 g/2 oz ground
almonds
50 g/2 oz flaked almonds
2 tbls brandy

Put the dried fruit into a bowl with the candied peel. Rinse and halve the cherries and add to the bowl, along with the sherry or orange juice. Mix, then cover and leave for 1–2 days, stirring once or twice each day.

Line a 20 cm/8 inch round cake tin with a double layer of greaseproof paper, and tie a double layer of newspaper around the outside of the tin. Set the oven to 140°C/275°F/Gas Mark 1.

Sift together the flours, baking powder and spices. Cream the butter or margarine with the sugar until light and fluffy; then, beat the eggs in a little at a time, adding some of the flour mixture if there is any sign of curdling. Fold in the flour mixture, then stir in the fruit, orange and lemon rinds, and the ground and flaked almonds. Add a little more liquid. Spoon the mixture into the cake tin and bake for 4–4½ hours, until a skewer inserted into the middle of the cake comes out clean. Stand the cake in its tin on a wire rack to cool.

Remove the cake from the tin, strip off the paper, prick the cake all over with a skewer, and pour the brandy over it. Wrap in greaseproof paper and store in an airtight tin until needed. It will keep well for 1–3 months and 'mature' during that time. Sprinkle a little more brandy over the top occasionally if you like during storage.

MAKES ONE 20 CM/8 INCH ROUND CAKE

ALMOND PASTE

200 g/7 oz ground
almonds
200 g/7 oz caster sugar
200 g/7 oz icing sugar
1 tbls lemon juice
2 eggs, beaten
a few drops of almond
essence

Put the almonds into a large bowl with the caster sugar, then sift in the icing sugar. Add the lemon juice, then gradually mix in the beaten eggs, adding enough to make a stiff paste. Don't knead the mixture too much or it may get oily.

MAKES ABOUT 700 G/1½ LB ENOUGH FOR A 20 CM/8 INCH CAKE

TO PUT THE PASTE ON THE CAKE

First prepare the jam mixture for coating the cake to make the almond paste stick. If you are using apricot jam, sieve it into a small saucepan, or use redcurrant or other jelly which avoids the need for sieving. Add a tablespoonful of water and heat gently until melted.

Use two-thirds of the almond paste to roll out a strip the height of the cake and the same length as the cake's circumference. Gather up the trimmings, and roll these, and the remaining almond paste, to make a circle just slightly larger than the top of the cake. You might prefer to use the cake upside down, as the base is usually flatter than the top. Brush this with some of the melted jam or jelly – don't do the sides yet. Holding the cake by the sides, put it, jammy-side down, on to the circle of almond paste. Now turn it up the right way, brush the sides with jam and, holding the top and bottom of the cake between your flat hands, place the side of the cake on the strip of almond paste and simply roll it along – the almond paste will stick to it.

Gently press together the join where the ends meet, then put the cake on a board and leave to dry for 24 hours.

OPPOSITE: (left) Traditional Christmas Cake with Royal Icing and (right) Traditional Christmas Cake with Fondant Icing (page 12)

ROYAL ICING

2 egg whites
2 tsp glycerine

700 g/1½ lb icing sugar,
sifted, plus extra for
dusting
juice of ½ small lemon

Beat the egg whites and glycerine together, then add the icing sugar, a little at a time, beating well after each addition. After adding half the icing sugar, add the lemon juice. Continue adding the remaining icing sugar, beating to incorporate, until the mixture forms stiff peaks.

MAKES ENOUGH FOR A 20 CM/8 INCH ROUND CAKE

VEGAN VERSION

For vegan icing, use a thick glacé icing (page 134).

TO ROYAL ICE THE CAKE

Spoon the icing on to the cake, on top of the almond paste. Use a spatula to draw the icing thickly and evenly all over the top and sides, then use it to flick up decorative peaks.

To decorate the Royal Icing Cake to the left in the photograph, I swirled about 12 thin red ribbons around the candle centrepiece, curling them so that they fell prettily over the cake. As a finishing touch, I arranged some holly sprigs (and berries) at intervals around the top outside edge, and tied a red ribbon round the sides.

FONDANT ICING

450 g/1 lb icing sugar,
sifted
50 g/2 oz liquid glucose

1 egg white
icing sugar for dusting

Mix all the ingredients together to make a stiff, mouldable paste. (If you wish, you can use bought fondant icing, in which case, you will need 2 × 450 g/ 1 lb packets to cover the cake.)

MAKES ENOUGH TO ICE AND DECORATE A 20 CM/8 INCH ROUND CAKE

TO FONDANT ICE THE CAKE

Roll the icing out, using sifted icing sugar to dust if necessary, to make a piece large enough to cover the top and sides of the cake. Lift this up carefully by putting your flat hands underneath it, then gently lower it over the cake, letting it fall down the sides. Ease the icing round the sides of the cake and press it gently into position. Trim all the extra icing away. Leave for 6–8 hours.

Meanwhile, gather up all the trimmings which you can colour if you like, re-roll and cut into interesting shapes with pastry cutters to decorate the top and sides of the cake.

For the Fondant Icing Cake on the right of our photograph, I cut out holly shapes and arranged them around the top outside edge of the cake and around the base, on the silver cake board. To add to the festive feeling, I put some small silver cake-decorating balls on top of each holly 'leaf' and some real holly leaves in a circle in the centre, surrounding the Christmas candle.

The final touch (beside each leaf) are the special Christmas jasmine flowers. To make them, use a fine brush to paint fresh jasmine flowers with a lightly whisked egg white (just enough to break it up – add a drop or two of water if it's too viscous). Then lightly sprinkle with caster sugar and leave to dry at room temperature or in a very cool oven. Just before serving, tie a ribbon round the cake to complete the decoration.

OTHER IDEAS FOR FONDANT ICING

Decorate the sides and top of the cake with interesting fondant shapes – and paint them with cake colourings. Angels round the sides with one on top would be appropriately festive; or you could stamp out lots of Christmas stars and scatter them over the top and sides of the cake.

A favourite fondant idea of mine is to ice the cake, then cut out some green fondant leaves (use green cake colouring to get the right colour) to go in the centre. Put a red candle in the middle of the 'leaves' and, around it, Christmas roses, also made from fondant icing. It's quite easy to mould them – stick five white 'petals' round a gold 'stamen' with egg white; about five 'roses' should fit nicely around the candle. Finish with a red ribbon around the centre.

OTHER CAKE DECORATIONS

You could use almond paste on its own. Flute it attractively around the top of the cake (as you'd flute a pie), perhaps lightly score in a criss-cross pattern with a knife. Then arrange a candle and holly, or marzipan fruit, in the centre and tie a toning ribbon round the outside.

Or try a jewel-bright topping of crystallized fruits and brazilnuts, halved pecans and whole cashew nuts or blanched almonds. Stick these on to the top of the cake in an attractive pattern with warmed clear honey, and brush over with more warmed honey to glaze. For a sparkling finish, brush over the whole cake with clear honey, then sprinkle with preserving sugar or even some coloured coffee sugar and little silver balls.

PLANNING AND PREPARATION

14

VEGETARIAN CHRISTMAS PUDDING

100 g/4 oz plain wholewheat flour
1 tsp baking powder
100 g/4 oz pure vegetable fat
100 g/4 oz dark brown sugar
450 g/1 lb mixed dried fruit
100 g/4 oz candied peel, chopped

100 g/4 oz soft breadcrumbs
25 g/1oz flaked almonds
grated rind of 1 orange
grated rind of 1 lemon
½ tsp ground ginger
½ tsp grated nutmeg
1½ tsp mixed spice
1 tbls black treacle
4 tbls whisky
150 ml/5 fl oz stout

Sift the flour and baking powder on to a plate and leave on one side. Put the fat and sugar into a large bowl and beat until creamy, then add all the remaining ingredients, including the flour, and mix very well, to a thick, creamy consistency. (Don't forget to wish!) Cover the bowl and leave overnight.

Next day, put the mixture into a lightly greased 1.2 l/2 pint basin (or two 600 ml/1 pint basins), cover with a circle of greased greaseproof paper and put on a lid if the basin has one. If it doesn't secure with some foil, or a pudding cloth, over the top of the basin. Steam for 6–8 hours. (The longer a pudding is steamed the darker and more richly flavoured it will become.) Cool, then put a clean piece of greaseproof and new foil or a fresh pudding cloth on top of the bowl, and store the pudding in a cool dry place until required.

Steam for a further 3 hours before eating.
SERVES 6

TO FLAME A CHRISTMAS PUDDING
The important thing is to warm the brandy first. Put 4 tablespoons of brandy – or 2 tablespoons brandy and 2 tablespoons vodka, which is higher in alcohol so burns well – into a metal soup ladle and warm by holding over a gas flame or electric ring. Then quickly light the brandy and pour carefully over and round the pudding.

OPPOSITE: *Vegetarian Christmas Pudding, flamed with brandy*

MINCEMEAT

You can vary the ingredients in this deliciously moist and spicy mincemeat to suit your taste. If you don't like cherries, for instance, increase the amount of mixed dried fruit, or use 100 g/ 4 oz delicious Lexia raisins instead.

450 g/1 lb fresh ripe pears, peeled and chopped
grated rind of 1 lemon
grated rind of 1 orange
450 g/1 lb mixed dried fruit
100 g/4 oz whole candied peel, chopped

100 g/4 oz glacé cherries, halved
100 g/4 oz dates, chopped
50 g/2 oz flaked almonds
1 tsp mixed spice
½ tsp grated nutmeg
½ tsp ground ginger
4 tbls whisky

Mix all the ingredients together in a large bowl, and set to one side for 1–2 hours to allow the flavours to mingle. Store in an airtight jar until ready to use.
MAKES 1 KG/2½ LB – ENOUGH TO MAKE ABOUT 25–30 PIES

MINCE PIES

1 quantity rich shortcrust pastry (see page 29)
450 g/1 lb mincemeat
caster sugar

Set the oven to 200°C/400°F/Gas Mark 6 and lightly grease a shallow 12-hole bun tin. On a lightly floured board, roll out the pastry thinly then cut out twelve 7.5 cm/3 inch circles and twelve 6 cm/2½ inch circles using a round cutter. Press one of the larger circles gently into each section of the bun tin, then put a teaspoonful of mincemeat on top and cover with the smaller pastry circles. Don't fill them too full, or they may ooze and burst as they cook. Press down at the edges, make a steamhole in the top, then bake for about 20 minutes, or until the pastry is lightly browned. Cool in the tin.

Freeze until required. Serve warm, sprinkled with caster sugar.
MAKES 12 PIES

MAKING THE MOST OF YOUR FREEZER

I find it a help to make, about six weeks in advance if I'm organised, a rough menu plan for the main meals to be cooked over the Christmas period so that I can freeze some of the dishes (as many as I have time to do) in advance. If you make your menu plan and list of dishes for the freezer in good time, it's easier and more enjoyable to fit in the extra cooking over the 4–6 weeks leading up to Christmas. You'll find ideas for menus for different types of meals on page 18 (The Twelve Days of Christmas), as well as notes of the individual recipes that freeze well in other parts of the book. Some of the most useful standbys for the freezer are listed below.

DIPS AND FIRST COURSES

These are the last thing you want to be bothered with when you're busy, so having some of these frozen is a real help. Dips such as hummus and aubergine freeze well (others, like soured cream and avocado, don't but can be whizzed up in moments). Most soups freeze beautifully, and it's particularly handy to have a supply of special garnishes, such as crisp Sesame Stars (served with Cream of Carrot Soup on page 99) or croûtons. Home-made Vegetable Stock is another good standby. Although there are some quite good stock cubes and powders on the market, nothing can compare with the delicacy of home-made stock, and if I haven't got any, I tend to use water. One way of getting good stock without any bother is to save the water in which vegetables have been cooked. I keep this, covered, in a jug in the fridge or freeze some if there's extra.

SAUCES

Sauces are a most useful freezer item, often enabling you to create a meal from a few ingredients you happen to have in, or providing the finishing touch to a meal without much effort. I find you can never have too much Fresh Tomato Sauce or Italian Tomato Sauce in the freezer. Thaw, heat and serve with pasta and you have a filling meal in minutes; spread on top of any number of different bases, such as French bread, baps or round pitta breads, top with slices of tomato, pepper, mushroom, or whatever you fancy and grated cheese and a few black olives for quick pizzas; pour over lightly cooked vegetables, such as fennel, top with Parmesan cheese and serve as a light main course; or serve with a vegetarian burger, croquette or savoury loaf to add lots of colour and moisture to the meal.

Traditional Christmas Sauces – Bread Sauce, Cranberry Sauce and Gravy (vegetarian style, of course) – all freeze perfectly, and if you're planning to serve these, it's a great help to get them done in advance. The same applies to sweet sauces and accompaniments such as Brandy Butter, Rum Sauce, Vegan Cream and Coulis.

VEGETABLES AND HERBS

On the whole, I prefer to use fresh vegetables for accompaniments, although there are some exceptions. It's always useful to have some Red and Green Peppers (page 61) in the freezer, either for a salad or to incorporate into another dish. Festive Red Cabbage (page 45) also freezes well and is a useful dish for the freezer because it's good with many savoury dishes. Make it into a light main meal with the addition of roast, baked or mashed potatoes, and perhaps some cooked chestnuts. Dishes that can be cooked straight from frozen are particularly useful so I always try to keep a stock – Light Gratin Dauphinois and Parsley Potato Stars (page 38) are two favourites in this category. In addition to all of these, I like to keep a stock of plain vegetables such as petit pois, sweetcorn, green beans, broad beans, leaf spinach and, sorry to admit this, oven chips. Chopped parsley is another good standby – in fact, most herbs freeze well and could be stashed away for times when they're difficult to find fresh.

OPPOSITE: *Cream of Carrot Soup with Sesame Stars, page 99*

BREAD AND PASTRY

Home-made rolls keep well in the freezer, as of course does any commercial bread. I like to keep a supply of our normal favourite wholewheat loaf, plus specials like baguettes, croissants, pitta bread, perhaps some Italian Ciabatta bread. White and wholewheat bread-crumbs, stored in polythene bags which can be topped up whenever you have bread over, are always useful to have, but especially so when you're making Christmas recipes. And if you like Garlic Bread it's a great help to have some prepared and wrapped in foil ready for baking. Don't do too far in advance – no more than 1–2 weeks – the flavour of garlic mysteriously decreases in the freezer.

A packet of filo and home-made or bought puff pastry is handy to have, too, and I like to store flan/tart cases either uncooked or, more convenient, baked blind, for finishing with a quickly made filling. Many of the savoury pastry dishes in this book can also be frozen (see below and on the recipe pages for specific suggestions).

MAIN COURSE DISHES

What main course dishes you put in your freezer depends very much on your own taste and your menu plans. I find it useful to have some kind of frozen burgers (such as Kate's Butterbean Croquettes – page 50), so that I can take them out individually for giving kids suppers and snacks at odd times. They can be cooked quickly from frozen. Terrines, savoury bakes and loaves are also useful and can be frozen raw, cooked or partially cooked. They're best thawed before cooking.

Savoury pastry dishes such as Flaky Mushroom Christmas Tree (page 50), Chestnut and Red Wine Pâté en Croûte (page 82), and Christmas Savoury Strudel (page 95) freeze excellently; open-freeze them before baking, then wrap them well to protect any fragile garnishes. To use, loosen their wrappings and let them thaw completely, then bake as described in the recipe.

PUDDINGS

Ice creams and sorbets are useful freezer basics, and can be quickly made more special if you serve them with your own frozen fruit coulis or supply of purées and some thin, crisp biscuits or tuilles; or, a favourite with my children (as well as with adults), Meringue Nests. Already-made meringues are a particularly useful extra to have available at Christmas. Other made-up puddings will depend on your menus, but Chocolate Charlotte (page 110) as well as traditional Buche de Noel (page 132) freeze well, as do most cheesecakes and traditional old-fashioned trifles. I find it useful to keep one or two sweet pastry dishes over and above mince pies as they are so popular with my family – the Gooseberry Tartlets (page 106) fit this bill; they are wildly out of season, and add a pleasantly refreshing contrast to the usual Christmas flavours.

CAKES

I'm not keen on giving up freezer space to foods which store well in other ways, so I never keep rich fruit cakes or gingerbread in the freezer, although both are good for Christmas. Both can be made in advance and kept in a tin, as can lighter cakes such as Madeira Cake (page 129), Vegan Chocolate Sponge Cake (page 128), Light Ginger Cake with Lemon Icing (page 131), if they're made just before you want them; but if you want to get ahead with these they freeze very well and can be made and decorated before freezing – open-freeze them so that they are hard before you wrap them, and pack them carefully to avoid damage.

THE TWELVE DAYS OF CHRISTMAS . . .

Christmas Eve though not, strictly speaking, one of the traditional 'twelve days', is, for most of us, the start of Christmas, as friends and family gather for this very special, and I think rather magical, night of the year.

The planning of the meal on Christmas Eve will, of course, depend on circumstances: whether people are arriving late, from far away, perhaps; whether you're planning to go to Midnight Mass . . . In some families, the food on this night is as traditional as Christmas Dinner. I feel that the ideal meal for Christmas Eve is something festive, but different enough from Christmas Dinner not to rival it. Also, since however well organised you are Christmas Eve always seems to be a busy time of last-minute shopping, present-wrapping and beginning the preparations for Christmas Day, it should either be fairly easy to make, or something which you can freeze in advance and just heat through.

A meal which I think meets all these criteria is Christmas Eve Couscous (page 52). This consists of several bowls of different mixtures: the grain (couscous), the lightly spiced, colourful vegetable stew, and as many extras – such as chick peas, raisins, chutneys and pickles, pine nuts – that you want to serve. You can pass the bowls around the table and everyone can help themselves, which gets things off to a friendly start and somehow adds to the feeling of celebration. This meal is easy to do but all the extras make it look as if you've taken a good deal more trouble than you have. A simple first course, such as Stuffed Vine Leaves (page 32), or a dip like guacamole with some crisp fresh vegetables or warm pitta bread, go well with this, as does a pudding such as Orange Slices with Flower Water (page 112). If people are going to church, you might like to save the pudding for later and make it something warming and substantial to eat on their return like hot Mince Pies, for instance, or Swedish Ring Cake (page 134). Or serve some good chunky bread or home-made biscuits with a good selection of cheese and pickles, nuts and fruit.

One of the Christmas Dinner menus in this book would also be ideal for a special Christmas Eve meal – I've given quite a variety of suggestions in a later chapter, so it's quite possible to use one on Christmas Eve and another, different one, for Christmas Day itself. Round the meal off with a light and delicious pudding such as an ice cream bombe, Rum-Marinated Fruits with Coconut and Lime Cream (page 116) or Lemon and Ginger Cheesecake (page 116). Another meal I'm fond of is the Flaky Mushroom Christmas Tree (page 50) with its fresh and tangy creamy herb sauce; or, for a festive yet light meal, I also very much like Chestnut-Stuffed Mushrooms (page 45) served with Festive Red Cabbage (page 45) and Potatoes with Lemon (page 37), or my own version of the French classic creamy Light Gratin Dauphinois (page 38).

It's a good idea to decide on your Christmas Dinner menu – the most important meal of the year –

first, before you plan any of the others, and choose your other meals accordingly. There are lots of ideas for this in the Christmas Dinner chapter, and each menu comes complete with countdown timetables to make sure that everything goes really smoothly, and that you enjoy the meal as much as everyone else. Whether you have Christmas Dinner at lunchtime or in the evening, you will probably want something light for the other meal of the day. My family is incurably traditional; having known only vegetarian Christmases, they always want the most traditional of vegetarian meals on Christmas Day: Cashew Nut Roast served with roast potatoes, gravy, cranberry sauce and all the other trimmings (page 78) – and they want it at lunchtime, followed by the Queen's speech and present-opening under the tree. I make enough of the roast to have it sliced cold in the evening with salad and pickles, followed by trifle, ice cream or hot mince pies.

Other ideas for a light-yet-Christmassy second meal of the day would be Festive Spring Rolls (page 32) (which can be frozen); Tagliatelle with Creamy Walnut Sauce (page 46), both of which I'd serve with a simple salad – mixed leaf, shredded lettuce or lettuce heart, for instance. If you're feeling really full, several dips of different colours, with some fresh vegetables, such as radishes, spring onions and slices of lettuce heart, plus some bread, biscuits, crisps or tortilla chips, can be surprisingly successful and great fun to eat.

On the days following Christmas, fresh, light food seems to be what people fancy most – and it must either be quick and easy to make or eminently freezable. Some of our favourites are Clear Watercress Soup (page 36); Lemony Vegetables (page 41), served with light and creamy mashed potatoes or mixed rice; my daughter Kate's Butterbean Croquettes (page 50) or Little Brie and Hazelnut Bakes (page 67), both of which are delicious with some fruity home-made cranberry sauce; Avocado with Curried Brazilnut Stuffing (page 51); and Fennel Parmesan (page 38), which has a good, clean flavour. Puddings which are particularly good at this time are Lemon and Ginger Cheesecake (page 116); the refreshing Christmas Dried Fruit Salad (page 112); or Lychee Sorbet (page 115).

CHRISTMAS TIMETABLE

 **OCTOBER**

- Find recipes for Christmas Cake, Pudding and Mincemeat.

- Make lists of ingredients needed and start buying items which store well, such as dried fruit.

- Check equipment: now is the time to buy new tins (the stronger and heavier the better), pudding basins, pastry cutters or anything special needed in Christmas recipes.

- Save jars for the mincemeat (and any other Christmas preserves).

- Check supplies of foil (the narrow type is most convenient), nonstick and greaseproof paper, polythene bags, clingfilm and labels for the freezer.

- If you're expecting to have a large party at Christmas and have limited freezer space, collect polystyrene boxes and packing, and get some freezer ice packs – these are good for keeping food cold for short periods of time when the fridge and freezer are full.

- Clear out the freezer and start using any items which need eating up to give you plenty of freezer space for Christmas.

OCTOBER/NOVEMBER

- Make the Christmas Cake, Pudding and Mincemeat. Keep them in a cool, dry place.

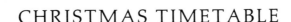 **NOVEMBER**

- Think about Christmas menus and any special dishes you want to try; check that you have the equipment needed.

- Make a plan of dishes to prepare for the freezer, and a rough timetable; most dishes keep well in the freezer for 4–6 weeks.

- Make any preserves, such as Kumquats in Brandy (page 144) or Mixed Vegetables in Oil (page 142), for eating at Christmas or giving as presents.

- From mid-November onwards, you can start freezing dishes for Christmas.

 **DECEMBER**

- The more you can get into the freezer during the first fortnight the better.

- Make and freeze Mince Pies, Brandy Butter, Rum Sauce (see recipes in this chapter).

- Finalise Christmas Dinner menu. Make and freeze main courses and sauces as applicable. Some first courses, such as Iced Melon Soup with Violets can be frozen, too.

- During the second week, put almond paste and icing on your Christmas cake.

OPPOSITE: *Iced Melon Soup with Violets, page 82*

20

VEGETABLE STOCK

900 g/2 lb mixed
vegetables, for instance,
2 onions, 3 sticks of
celery, 2 carrots,
1 turnip, 2 broccoli
stalks
25 g/1 oz butter or white
vegetable fat

5 garlic cloves — no need
to peel, just halve
12 peppercorns
2 bay leaves
bunch of parsley, or just
the stalks
a few sprigs of thyme, or
1 tsp dried

Scrub and roughly chop the vegetables. Melt the butter or fat in a large saucepan, add the vegetables and fry for 10 minutes until soft. Add 1.5 l/2½ pints of water, the garlic, peppercorns, bay leaves, parsley and thyme. Bring to the boil, cover, and simmer very gently for about 40 minutes, until the vegetables are very soft. Leave the pot to stand until it's completely cold, then skim the fat from the surface. This stock keeps for a few days in the fridge and also freezes well: old cream or yogurt cartons make good containers.
MAKES ABOUT 1–1.25 L/2–2¼ PINTS

FRESH TOMATO SAUCE

Even in winter when tomatoes don't have that warm, sun-drenched flavour, I prefer this sauce to the more strongly flavoured kind made from canned tomatoes (see opposite), although both are useful. This one is good for serving with delicately flavoured foods, and my children love it with pasta of any shape! It's also good with boiled rice tossed with a few fresh herbs. In fact, I find I can't make too much of it. You can vary the basic sauce by adding chopped fresh herbs (basil and oregano are particularly good), sliced button mushrooms, crushed garlic or a dash of red wine.

1 medium-sized onion,
finely chopped
1 tbls olive oil

1 kg/2 lb 2 oz tomatoes,
skinned and roughly
chopped
salt and freshly ground
black pepper

In a large saucepan, fry the onion in the oil for 10 minutes, until soft but not browned. Add the tomatoes and cook for about 10 minutes, until they are soft but still bright in colour and fresh in flavour. Season with salt and pepper and freeze until required.

Usually I serve this sauce just as it is, which is fine for pasta and simple dishes, although it can be puréed in a food processor and then strained quickly through a sieve if you want a smooth sauce. Ideally it would be useful to keep both types, the chunky and the smooth, in the freezer!
SERVES 6

ITALIAN TOMATO SAUCE

This sauce has a stronger flavour which some people may prefer. I find it particularly useful as a topping for home-made pizzas. Spoon it on top of any bases which happen to be handy; home-made bread ones if there's time, otherwise split and toasted rolls or muffins, round pitta bread, or slices of bread which have been dried out in a cool oven, like the bases of Italian crostini.

1 onion, chopped
2 tbls olive oil
2 garlic cloves, crushed
2 × 400 g/14 oz cans
tomatoes
½ tsp dried basil

½ tsp dried oregano
1 bay leaf
150 ml/5 fl oz red wine,
stock or water
salt and freshly ground
black pepper

In a large saucepan, fry the onion in the oil for 10 minutes, until soft but not browned. Add the garlic, tomatoes and juice, basil, oregano, bay leaf and the wine, stock or water. Cook gently for 20 minutes, until the tomatoes have almost reduced to a purée. Remove the bay leaf, then purée the sauce in a blender or food processor. Season with salt and pepper. A little extra liquid can be added at this point for a thinner sauce. Freeze until required.
SERVES 6

CRANBERRY SAUCE

100 g/4 oz cranberries,   *50 g/2 oz sugar*
  washed and picked over   *1 tbls port or orange juice*
3 tbls water   *(optional)*

Put the cranberries into a saucepan with the water. Bring to the boil, then simmer until the berries are tender; about 4–5 minutes. Add the sugar and cook gently until dissolved.

    Remove from the heat and add the port or orange juice, if you're using these. Either serve warm or freeze until required.
SERVES 6

BREAD SAUCE

3 cloves   *15 g/½ oz butter*
1 onion, peeled   *2 tbls cream*
300 ml/½ pint milk   *salt and freshly ground*
1 bay leaf   *black pepper*
50 g/2 oz white bread,   *grated nutmeg*
  crusts removed

Stick the cloves into the onion, then put the onion into a saucepan with the milk and bay leaf. Bring to the boil, then take off the heat, add the bread, cover and leave on one side for 15–30 minutes to allow the flavours to infuse.

    Remove the onion and the bay leaf. Beat the mixture to break up the bread, and stir in the butter, cream and salt, pepper and grated nutmeg to taste. Either serve warm or freeze until required.
SERVES 6

VEGAN VERSION
Use vegan margarine instead of butter, soya milk instead of milk and omit the cream.

BECHAMEL SAUCE

This sauce will keep, well covered, in the fridge, for at least a few days.

25 g/1 oz butter   *6 black peppercorns*
25 g/1 oz flour   *a sprig of thyme*
600 ml/1 pint milk   *1–2 blades of mace*
piece of onion, celery and   *salt and freshly ground*
  scraped carrot   *black pepper*
1 bay leaf   *grated nutmeg*

Melt the butter in a large saucepan. Add the flour, stir over the heat for a couple of minutes, then add the milk, a quarter at a time, mixing well between each addition. Add the onion, celery, carrot, bay leaf, peppercorns, thyme and mace and leave to simmer gently for 10–15 minutes. Strain the sauce through a sieve into a clean saucepan. Season with salt, pepper and grated nutmeg, and use as appropriate, with vegetables, pasta or other savouries.
MAKES 450 ML/¾ PINT

VEGAN VERSION
Use vegan margarine instead of butter and soya milk instead of dairy milk.

PARSLEY SAUCE
Add 2–4 tablespoons chopped parsley and a few drops of lemon juice (to taste) to the sauce after straining.

You may wish to make more Cranberry Sauce than the quantities given here, for serving with several meals over Christmas. Freeze in suitable sized containers and reheat gently before serving.

GARLIC BREAD

I love crisp, hot, buttery garlic bread and could eat it with almost any soup or salad. Assuming that others share my passion, I find it very useful to have some loaves already spread with butter, wrapped in foil and stored in the freezer, ready to pop straight into the oven. I've given quantities for one normal-size French stick here, but I generally make up more while I'm about it. It's sometimes convenient to freeze the bread in smaller amounts, perhaps a quarter of a loaf, firmly wrapped in foil. As the garlic flavour lessens during freezing, it's best not to keep it for more than 3–4 weeks, and 1–2 weeks is better.

1 French stick	*2–4 fat garlic cloves,*
75 g/3 oz soft butter or	*crushed*
vegan margarine	

Cut the stick into 2.5 cm/1 inch diagonal slices without cutting right through to the base. Mash the butter with the garlic until it's thoroughly blended, then spread both sides of each slice of bread with the butter mixture. Press the loaf together and wrap in foil – or make two packages if this is more convenient and will fit your oven better. To use immediately, bake at 200°C/400°F/Gas Mark 6 for 20 minutes, or until it's hot inside and crisp on the outside; or freeze until required, then bake from frozen allowing 30 minutes.

————————— —————————

FLAVOURED BUTTERS

Flavoured butters are a useful way of adding extra interest to vegetables and other dishes. Try parsley or lemon butter on top of plain steamed carrots, curry butter on boiled parsnips or spread on bread when making croûtons (see page 58), and paprika butter on open mushrooms before grilling.

(see page 58)

OPPOSITE: *Garlic Bread with Paprika, Parsley and Lemon Butters*

PARSLEY BUTTER

75 g/3 oz soft butter	*2 tbls finely chopped*
	parsley

Beat the butter until creamy, then mix in the chopped parsley. Other herbs can also be used – chopped chives are good. Chill until firm, then wrap in foil and freeze until required.

LEMON BUTTER

75 g/3 oz soft butter	*finely grated rind and*
	juice of ½ lemon

Beat the butter until creamy, then mix in the lemon rind and juice. Chill until firm, then wrap in foil and freeze until required.

CURRY BUTTER

1 tbls olive oil	*75 g/3 oz soft butter*
2 tsp curry powder	

Heat the oil in a small pan, then add the curry powder and stir over the heat for a few seconds, to release the flavour. Cool, then beat this into the soft butter. More or less curry powder can be used according to taste. Chill until firm, then wrap in foil and freeze until required.

PAPRIKA BUTTER

2 tsp paprika	*75 g/3 oz soft butter*
1 tbls lemon juice	

Beat the butter until creamy, then mix in the paprika and lemon juice. Chill until firm, then wrap in foil and freeze until required.

BRANDY BUTTER

100 g/4 oz unsalted	*100 g/4 oz soft brown*
butter	*sugar or icing sugar*
	2 tbls brandy

Cream the butter and sugar or icing sugar together until the mixture is fluffy, then beat in the brandy. Spoon into a serving dish, cover and chill until firm, then wrap in foil and freeze until required.
SERVES 6

Use vegan margarine for vegan flavoured 'butters'.

VEGAN CREAM

3 tsp cornflour
150 ml/5 fl oz
   unsweetened soya milk
1 vanilla pod

95 g/3½ oz soft pure
   vegetable margarine
2–3 tsp icing sugar
a few drops of vanilla
   extract (optional)

In a small bowl, blend the cornflour to a paste with a little of the soya milk. Put the rest of the milk into a saucepan with the vanilla pod and bring to the boil, pour over the cornflour mixture, stir, and return to the pan. Stir until the mixture thickens, then remove from the heat and leave until completely cold.

In another bowl, beat the margarine until it's light and creamy, then gradually whisk in the cooled cornflour mixture, avoiding the vanilla pod, which can be rinsed, dried and used again. It's important to add the cornflour mixture gradually, whisking well, to produce a beautiful light whipped cream. Add the icing sugar towards the end, a teaspoonful at a time, tasting the mixture to get it just right.

The delicate vanilla flavour can be enhanced with a drop or two of vanilla extract, or you can add a dash of brandy or rum, or orange or rose flower water, depending on what you're serving it with.
SERVES 4–6

MERINGUE NESTS

2 egg whites
pinch of cream of tartar

100 g/4 oz caster sugar

Set the oven to 150°C/300°F/Gas Mark 2 and draw six 7.5 cm/3 inch circles well apart on greaseproof or nonstick paper. Place on a baking sheet, grease with butter or cooking oil and sprinkle with flour.

Put the egg whites into a clean, grease-free bowl with the cream of tartar and whisk until stiff and dry. (You should be able to turn the bowl upside down without the egg whites falling out!) Whisk in half the sugar then add the remaining sugar and whisk well.

Put the mixture into a piping bag fitted with a large shell nozzle and pipe circles round and round within the circles, then a final circle on top of the outermost circle, to form a nest shape.

Put the meringues into the oven, then reduce the setting to 110°C/200°F/Gas Mark ¼ and bake for 1½–2 hours, or until they are dried out. Turn the oven off and leave them to cool in the oven. Remove the meringues from the baking sheet with a palette knife. Either cool and use immediately or arrange carefully in a lidded container, cover and freeze until required.
MAKES 6

APRICOT COULIS

225 g/8 oz dried apricots   25 g/1 oz caster sugar

Put the apricots into a saucepan, cover with plenty of water and leave to soak overnight.

Next day, add the sugar and more water if necessary, so that the apricots are well covered. Bring to the boil, then let them simmer, uncovered, for about an hour, or until nearly all the water has gone and the apricots are very tender and bathed in a glossy syrup.

Cool, then liquidize thoroughly with some water to make a smooth purée. Add more water to thin the purée to a pouring consistency – like double cream, or even a bit thinner. Pour into suitable containers for freezing – old cream or yogurt cartons with a snap-on plastic lid are ideal, label and freeze. To use, simply thaw, then gently heat if you want to serve it hot.
SERVES 6

OPPOSITE: *Gooseberry Tartlets, page 106 with Apricot Coulis*

RASPBERRY COULIS

450 g/1 lb raspberries   2 tbls water
 (frozen are fine)   2 tbls caster sugar

Liquidize the raspberries with the water and sugar, then turn the mixture into a saucepan. Bring to the boil and boil for 1 minute, to make the sauce clear and glossy. Cool, then either serve warm or freeze as before until required.
SERVES 6

RUM SAUCE

25 g/1 oz butter or vegan   25 g/1 oz caster sugar
 margarine   4–6 tbls single cream
25 g/1 oz cornflour   2–3 tbls rum
600 ml/1 pint milk

Melt the butter or margarine in a medium-sized saucepan. Add the cornflour and stir for a few seconds before pouring in the milk, one third at a time, whisking well after each addition. Simmer for a couple of minutes, then stir in the sugar, cream and rum. Either use immediately or tip into a suitable container and freeze until required.
SERVES 6

RICH SHORTCRUST PASTRY

150 g/5 oz 85%   90 g/3½ oz butter
 wholewheat flour   1 egg yolk
pinch of salt   1 tbls water

OPPOSITE: *Flaky Mushroom Christmas Tree, page 50, made with Quick Flaky Pastry*

Sift the flour and salt into a bowl or food processor. Add the butter, cut into pieces, add the egg yolk and water, and either mix quickly together with a fork, or whizz for a few seconds without the plunger to let in more air, to make a medium-soft dough.

This pastry freezes excellently, both cooked and uncooked. To store, wrap loosely and freeze.
MAKES APPROX 250 G/9 OZ PASTRY

QUICK FLAKY PASTRY

250 g/9 oz strong brown   150 ml/5 fl oz ice-cold
 flour   water
1 tsp salt   squeeze of lemon juice
250 g/9 oz cold butter

Sift the flour and salt into a large bowl.

Cut the butter into 5 mm/¼ inch dice and add to the flour. Using a knife, mix the butter lightly into the flour so that the pieces just get coated with flour and are well distributed. Add the water and lemon juice and, again with a knife, quickly mix to a firm, soft dough.

On a lightly floured board, roll out into a rectangle, using short, quick movements, then fold the top over and over again. Give the folded pastry a quarter turn clockwise, so that the folded edges are now on your left. Roll again, sprinkling the pastry with some flour as necessary. Then fold and turn the pastry again. Keep repeating this rolling, folding and turning – the pastry we used in the picture of the Flaky Mushroom Christmas Tree (opposite) was rolled and turned seven times!

After the last rolling and folding, cover the pastry and chill it for at least 30 minutes. Or wrap loosely in foil and freeze until required. When you use, roll it out to about 2.5 mm/⅛ inch and bake in a hot oven preset to 230°C/450°F/Gas Mark 8 for 6–8 minutes, then reduce to 200°C/400°F/Gas Mark 6. Dampen the baking sheet, and remember to keep clear-cut edges for the pastry to rise from.
MAKES 350 G/12 OZ PASTRY

If you make the Rum Sauce in advance, cover with dots of butter to prevent a skin from forming.

LUNCHES, SUPPERS AND SNACKS

Although we tend to think in terms of Christmas cooking as being *the* Dinner, in fact for most of us it involves a great deal more, especially now that the Christmas holiday seems to last longer and longer, requiring, I've found, food which is special and festive, but which is also refreshing and a good contrast to Christmas Dinner and the traditional pudding, mince pies and cake. . . So the recipes in this section are for all the other meals that Christmas cooking involves, apart from the big day itself and parties.

As far as I'm concerned, such meals must either be quick and easy to make or good for freezing, so that they need the minimum of time and effort to produce on the day. I hope you'll agree that the dishes which follow meet these criteria. There are recipes for light savouries and dips, which can be used as starters or, with the addition of some salad and bread, become snack meals in themselves. The same applies to the soups,

which make particularly warming, filling winter meals, yet are easy on preparation and washing up.

   If there are young children in the party, it's helpful to have some dishes in the freezer which enable you to take out a small portion and heat it up when required, for giving the kids an early supper before they go to bed, or snacks at odd times to fit in with their routine. Parsley Potato Stars or Kate's Butterbean Croquettes come into this category, as do the Christmas Sacks and Father Christmas Faces — all can be frozen in individual quantities, and the latter can also be put together quickly from fresh (non-frozen) ingredients.

   Some of the recipes in this section could also be used for a vegetarian Christmas Dinner: the Flaky Mushroom Tree, perhaps served with traditional accompaniments from the Christmas Dinner chapter (pages 76 to 103), would be delightful, as would the Chestnut-Stuffed Mushrooms; or, for a real break from tradition, try the equally mouth-watering Avocados with Curried Brazilnut Stuffing.

STUFFED VINE LEAVES

Stuffed vine leaves make a delicious starter or party nibble, either on their own or with some thick Greek yogurt.

1 × 227 g/8 oz packet of preserved vine leaves
225 g/8 oz long-grain brown rice
1 large onion, chopped
2 tbls chopped parsley
2 tomatoes, skinned and chopped
50 g/2 oz pine kernels
50 g/2 oz raisins (optional)
½ tsp powdered cinnamon or allspice
2 garlic cloves, crushed
salt and freshly ground black pepper
6 tbls olive oil
150 ml/5 fl oz water
2 tbls lemon juice

Drain the vine leaves, cover them with cold water and leave to soak for 30 minutes or so, then rinse and drain them again, to remove some of the salt.

Blot the leaves dry, putting any torn ones aside. Half-fill a large saucepan with water, put in the rice and boil for 10 minutes, then drain and mix with the onion, parsley, tomatoes, pine kernels, raisins, if you're using them, cinnamon or allspice, garlic and seasoning. Put a spoonful of this mixture on each vine leaf, fold over the edges and roll the leaves up loosely, to allow space for the rice to swell.

Line a large frying pan with the torn leaves, then put in the stuffed vine leaves, side by side. Mix together the oil, water and lemon juice, and pour this over the leaves. Cover and cook over a very gentle heat for 2–2½ hours until the rice and leaves are tender. Keep an eye on the water level, and add a little more from time to time if necessary. Cool, then chill.

Serve cold.
MAKES ABOUT 36

When you're working with filo pastry, keep the rest of the pastry covered with polythene or a damp cloth to prevent it from drying out.

FESTIVE SPRING ROLLS

FOR THE SAUCE
2 large red peppers
2–4 large garlic cloves, peeled
salt and freshly ground black pepper
thin pepper slices, to garnish

FOR THE SPRING ROLLS
2 onions, chopped
2 carrots, diced

1 tbls olive oil
375 g/12 oz beansprouts
1 tsp grated fresh ginger
1 tbls Tamari
salt and freshly ground black pepper
1 × 375 g/12 oz filo pastry
extra olive oil for cooking
spring onion tassels and thin carrot curls, to garnish

First make the sauce, which can be done some time in advance and kept in the fridge. Quarter the peppers and remove the seeds. Place the peppers in a saucepan with the garlic cloves, cover with water and boil for 10–15 minutes, until the peppers are tender. Drain, liquidize, then pour the mixture through a sieve. Season with salt and pepper.

To make the spring rolls, if you're going to bake them straight away, set the oven to 200°C/400°F/ Gas Mark 6. In a frying pan, fry the onions and carrots in the oil for 7 minutes, until almost soft. Add the beansprouts and ginger and fry for a further 2–3 minutes, until all the vegetables are cooked. Add the Tamari and season with salt and pepper. Cool.

Cut a sheet of filo pastry in half, or divide it so that you have a piece measuring about 18 cm/7 inches square. Place a good heap of the mixture about 1cm/½ inch from the top and well clear of the sides, then fold over the top and the sides and roll up, to make a neat parcel. Place on a baking sheet which has been brushed with olive oil. Make the rest of the spring rolls in the same way and arrange on the baking sheet. Brush the spring rolls lightly with olive oil and bake for about 20 minutes, turning them over after about 10 minutes so that both sides get crisp.

Serve the rolls on individual plates on a pool of the red pepper sauce, garnished with spring onion, carrot and red pepper slices.
MAKES ABOUT 20 ROLLS

OPPOSITE: *Festive Spring Rolls*

WINTER VEGETABLE SOUP WITH ROUILLE AND CROÛTONS

The rouille on top of this soup adds a delicious, warming touch, but can be left off if you want a simpler version. You could stir in some soured cream or Greek yogurt instead, or top each bowlful with grated cheese, for a warming and filling winter meal.

1 large onion
2 leeks
225 g/8 oz celeriac or
 outer sticks of celery
2 tbls olive oil
1 × 400 g/14 oz can
 tomatoes in juice
1.2 l/2 pints water or
 vegetable stock
salt and freshly ground
 black pepper

FOR THE CROÛTONS
4 slices of wholewheat
 bread
25 g/1 oz butter

FOR THE ROUILLE
1 small or ½ large red
 pepper, seeded
1 red chilli, fresh or dried,
 seeded
50 g/2 oz white bread
100 ml/4 fl oz olive oil
salt and freshly ground
 pepper
chilli powder, to garnish

First make the croûtons, which can be done well in advance – they keep excellently in the freezer, too. Cut the crusts from the bread, then spread each side lightly with butter. Cut into small dice and place on a baking sheet. Set the oven to 150°C/300°F/Gas Mark 2 and bake for 40–60 minutes, or until they are crisp and crunchy.

Next, make the soup. Peel and chop the onion and clean, trim and slice the leeks, keeping as much of the green part as you can. Peel the celeriac and cut into 1 cm/½ inch dice or, if you are using celery, cut it into smaller dice as it takes a long time to soften. Heat the oil in a large saucepan, then put in all the vegetables. Cook over a gentle heat, with a lid on the pan, for 10–15 minutes, stirring every so often and not allowing them to brown. Add the tomatoes, with their liquid, and the water or stock, and bring to the boil. Then simmer gently for 30–40 minutes, or until all the vegetables are tender. Season with salt and pepper.

While the soup is cooking, make the rouille. Put the pepper into a pan of water and bring to the boil; simmer for about 10–15 minutes, or until the pepper is very tender, then drain thoroughly. Meanwhile, if you are using a dried chilli, soak this in a little boiling water. Put the cooked pepper, with any stalks removed, into a food processor with the fresh or soaked dried chilli, and whizz to a purée. Then add the bread, broken up into rough pieces, and whizz thoroughly, gradually adding the olive oil, whisking all the time, or after each addition. It's a bit like making mayonnaise, but much easier and less risky! As you add the oil, the mixture will thicken to a lovely smooth cream. Season with salt and a dash of chilli powder if you want it hotter. You can lighten the rouille mixture a bit by beating in a tablespoonful or two of boiling water if you wish.

Ladle the steaming hot soup into bowls and top each with a good spoonful of the rouille, some croûtons and a sprinkling of chilli powder – or let everyone help themselves to the extras.
SERVES 4

VARIATION
For a vivid yellow rouille, use a golden pepper instead of the red one.

OPPOSITE: *Winter Vegetable Soup with Rouille and Croûtons*

CAROL SINGERS' ONION SOUP

Surely this soup – a vegetarian version of the classic French Onion Soup – must be the most warming of them all? Wonderful to come in to on a cold night, whether you've been singing for your supper or not!

2 tbls oil
900 g/2 lb onions, thinly sliced
4 tsp sugar
salt and freshly ground black pepper
1.5 l/3 pints stock
2 garlic cloves, crushed
Tamari or Shoyu soy sauce
lemon juice
salt and freshly ground pepper
4–6 slices French stick
100 g/4 oz grated cheese

Heat the oil in a saucepan, add the onions and fry for 10 minutes or until they are tender but not browned. Add the sugar and some salt and pepper, and continue to fry for a further 15–20 minutes, until the onions become a deep golden brown. Don't let them burn! Add the stock and garlic, bring to the boil and let the soup simmer for about 10 minutes. Add Tamari or Shoyu soy sauce to taste, and a few drops of lemon juice, salt and pepper as necessary.

When you're ready to serve the soup, have some piping hot bowls ready. Put the French stick on a grill pan, top with the cheese, and grill for a few minutes, until the cheese has melted. Ladle the soup into the hot bowls, top each with a piece of cheesy bread, and serve at once.
SERVES 4–6

CLEAR WATERCRESS SOUP

This easy-to-make, refreshing soup is a good alternative to Celery and Stilton Soup in the Christmas Dinner on page 90, if you want something lighter, and vegan. Adding the watercress just before serving gives it a lovely bright colour and fresh flavour.

2 leeks
1 tbls olive oil
1 l/1¾ pints water or stock
1 × 75 g/3 oz packet watercress
Tamari or Shoyu soy sauce
salt and freshly ground pepper

Wash, trim and finely shred the leeks, using as much of the green part as you can. Heat the oil in a large saucepan, add the leeks, and fry gently for about 10 minutes, or until they are tender. Add the water or stock, bring to the boil, then simmer for about 10 minutes. Chop the watercress, then add this to the soup, along with Tamari or Shoyu to taste – probably 2–4 tablespoons. Season with a little salt and pepper if necessary. Reheat gently and serve.
SERVES 4–6

PASTA AND BROCCOLI BECHAMEL

225 g/8 oz broccoli
100 g/4 oz short macaroni, shells or other pasta shapes
300 ml/10 fl oz Bechamel Sauce (page 23)
salt and freshly ground black pepper
fresh breadcrumbs and a little butter or grated cheese for topping (optional)

Wash and trim the broccoli then divide it into smallish pieces. Cook it in 1 cm/½ inch of boiling water for 3–4 minutes, or until it is nearly tender. Drain and leave on one side.

Cook the pasta in a large panful of boiling water until that, too, is just tender – *al dente* – then drain it immediately.

Meanwhile, gently heat the bechamel sauce. Add the pasta and broccoli to the sauce, season, then stir gently over the heat until everything is really hot. Serve immediately or pour the mixture into a shallow heatproof dish, top with crumbs and a little butter or grated cheese and put under the grill until it's golden brown and crisp.
SERVES 2–3

VEGAN VERSION
Use a bechamel sauce made with soya milk and vegan margarine, and use margarine for the topping, if you're adding this.

CREAMY PARSNIP BAKE

This makes a pleasant, easy-going vegetable dish, which can be made in advance and reheated; I especially like it with any kind of crunchy burger, and it's also good for a light meal, with some watercress and sliced tomato.

900 g/2 lb parsnips	freshly grated nutmeg
25 g/1 oz butter	buttered crumbs or
150 ml/5 fl oz single	chopped walnuts or
cream	hazelnuts for topping
squeeze of lemon juice	(optional)
salt and freshly ground	
black pepper	

Peel the parsnips, then cut them into even-sized pieces. Put into a saucepan, cover with water, then bring to the boil and simmer, with a lid on the pan, until the parsnips are tender. Drain – the water makes good stock – then mash with the butter. When the parsnips are smooth, gradually beat in the cream.

Flavour with a squeeze of fresh lemon juice and salt, pepper and freshly grated nutmeg. You can then gently reheat the parsnip cream, stirring all the time over a gentle heat, and serve immediately; or you can spoon it into a shallow casserole, smooth the top, and sprinkle with some buttered crumbs or chopped walnuts or hazelnuts. It can then be reheated later in a moderate oven for 20–30 minutes, or in a microwave oven for 5–10 minutes.
SERVES 6

VEGAN VERSION
Use a vegan margarine instead of the butter, and soya milk instead of the cream. You could use a little extra vegan margarine to increase the richness – say 15 g/½ oz.

POTATOES WITH LEMON

The lemony tang is refreshing, and these potatoes are convenient to cook, because they can be prepared ready for baking, in advance, and don't need much attention once they're in the oven.

700 g/1½ lb potatoes	grated rind of 1 lemon
40 g/1½ oz melted butter	salt and freshly ground
or margarine	pepper

Choose even-sized potatoes and scrub them. Put them into a saucepan, cover with water and parboil them for 7 minutes or until they are almost tender. With a sharp knife, remove the skins and cut the potatoes in half lengthways. Melt the butter, then stir in the grated lemon rind. Brush this lemon butter all over the potatoes then put them in a single layer into a baking tin. Bake in the oven preset to 190°C/375°F/ Gas Mark 5, for about 45 minutes, or until they are golden and crisp, turning them over about half way through so they get evenly browned.
SERVES 6

You can use caraway instead of lemon rind in this way.

LIGHT GRATIN DAUPHINOIS

This lighter version of the delicious classic goes well with many of the savoury dishes in this book. I often serve it for a light meal with just a good crunchy mixed vegetable salad or some stir-fried vegetables (like Lemony Vegetables on page 41).

900 g/2 lb potatoes	*salt and freshly ground*
50 g/2 oz butter, melted	*black pepper*
1 garlic clove, crushed	*grated nutmeg*
1 onion, thinly sliced	*150 ml/5 fl oz single*
	cream

Set the oven to 180°C/350°F/Gas Mark 4.

Peel the potatoes and cut them into thin slices.

Grease a shallow wide gratin dish with half the butter, then spread the crushed garlic around the base and sides, too. Layer the potatoes and onion into the casserole, seasoning them with salt, nutmeg and freshly ground black pepper as you go, then pour over the cream and remaining butter. Cover with foil.

Bake for 1 hour, then remove the foil and bake for a further 30 minutes, or until golden brown.
SERVES 4

PARSLEY POTATO STARS

These are popular with children; they freeze well and can be grilled or baked from frozen.

900 g/2 lb potatoes	*salt and freshly ground*
25 g/1 oz butter	*pepper*
25 g/1 oz chopped	*grated nutmeg*
parsley	*flour*

Peel the potatoes and cut them into even-sized chunks, then boil in water to cover until they are tender. Drain really well, then dry a little over the heat. Mash with the butter, parsley and seasoning to taste, to make a smooth, very stiff consistency. Set the oven to 200°C/400°F/Gas Mark 6.

On a well-floured board, knead the mixture then press out to a depth of 1 cm/½ inch, and cut out star shapes. If you are using straight away, bake on a lightly oiled sheet for about 30 minutes until golden brown. If you are freezing them, bake for about 20 minutes until they are just set and beginning to brown, then cool and freeze.
SERVES 4–6

FENNEL PARMESAN

The slightly aniseed flavour of fennel makes it refreshing at any time, but particularly so, I think, at Christmas. This simple dish can be served as an accompanying vegetable, but I like it best as a simple lunch or supper, accompanied by a lovely big salad.

2 large fennel bulbs	*100 g/4 oz Parmesan*
	cheese, grated

Trim any tough outer leaves or stems from the fennel, then cut each bulb first in half and then into thin segments. Bring half a saucepanful of water to the boil, put in the fennel, and let it boil for 4 minutes or so, until it is just tender. Drain, keeping the liquid (which makes a delicious stock).

Heat the grill. Put the fennel in a single layer into a shallow flameproof dish and cover with the grated Parmesan cheese. Pour 6 tablespoons of the reserved liquid over the top of the cheese, then put the dish under a hot grill for about 5 minutes, or until the cheese has melted and browned lightly. Serve at once.
SERVES 4

OPPOSITE: *(top) Light Gratin Dauphinois and (bottom) Parsley Potato Stars*

LEMONY VEGETABLES

One of my favourite vegetable dishes, and a great hit with my family, this can be served as an accompanying vegetable, as a starter, or as a main course in its own right, perhaps with some cooked rice or a potato dish such as Light Gratin Dauphinois (page 38) or creamy mashed potatoes.

225 g/8 oz broccoli	1 lemon
175 g/6 oz mangetouts	1 bay leaf
2 onions	good pinch of dried thyme
2 red peppers	salt and freshly ground
1–2 fennel bulbs	black pepper
2 leeks	chopped parsley
75 ml/3 fl oz olive oil	

First prepare all the vegetables. Cut the thick stalks from the broccoli, then peel off the outer skin and cut the stalks into matchsticks. Separate the florets, halving any larger ones, so that they are all roughly the same size. Bring a large saucepan of water to the boil, put in the broccoli and blanch for 3 minutes, then drain into a colander and run under the cold tap. Pat dry with kitchen paper and leave on one side.

Top and tail the mangetouts, and blanch these in the same way for 1 minute; drain, refresh under cold water and pat dry. Peel and slice the onions; seed and slice the peppers; trim and slice the fennel into eighths or sixteenths, depending on the size of the bulbs; clean, trim and slice the leeks into 2.5 cm/1 inch lengths. (All this can be done in advance.)

When you are ready to make the dish, put the oil into a large saucepan or wok with the same quantity of water, the pared rind from half the lemon, the bay leaf and thyme. Put in the onions, red peppers, fennel and leeks and simmer for about 8 minutes, or until they are almost tender. Add the broccoli and mangetouts, and stir-fry for a further 2–3 minutes. Remove from the heat, add the grated rind of the other half of the lemon, and enough of the juice to give a pleasant tang. Season with salt and pepper, then serve, sprinkled with chopped parsley.

SERVES 4–6

OPPOSITE: *Lemony Vegetables*

SANTA'S SURPRISE PARCELS

The crêpes for this recipe can be made well in advance and frozen or kept in the fridge until needed. The following recipe makes 12 thin pancakes and each filling mixture is enough to fill about 4 pancakes.

FOR THE PANCAKES	1 tbls olive oil
50 g/2 oz plain white flour	2 eggs
50 g/2 oz plain wholemeal flour	300 ml/10 fl oz milk and water, mixed
good pinch of salt	oil for frying

To make the batter, if you have a food processor, simply put all the ingredients (except the oil for frying) into this; sift in the flours, as this helps to keep the mixture really light, and just tip in the final residue of bran from the sieve. Whizz without the plunger (to let in more air and lighten the pancakes), until everything is blended and you have a creamy mixture the consistency of double cream. Oil the base of a small frying pan (ideally measuring about 19 cm/7¼ inches across the top) with a pad of kitchen paper and a teaspoon of olive oil, then heat it until a small drop of water flicked into it splatters immediately.

Pour about 2 tablespoons of the batter mixture into the pan and immediately tip so that the batter spreads all over the base. If it doesn't spread well, it may be too thick, so mix in a little water. After a few seconds, when the bottom of the pancake is lightly browned and the top set, flip it over using a palette knife and your fingers, to cook the other side for a few seconds, then lift it out on to a large piece of greaseproof paper.

Continue to cook more crêpes in this way until all the mixture is used, putting them side by side on the greaseproof paper. You will probably need to regrease the frying pan after every 2–3 crêpes. Leave them to cool completely, then cut the paper between them and stack the pancakes, on their paper, on top of each other. Keep in the fridge or freeze until required.

Serve with a selection of the fillings listed overleaf.

Make the fillings for these crêpes ahead of time, and you have a meal in minutes.

41

FOR VEGAN CRÊPES

Omit the eggs; add 3 tablespoons chick pea flour and a teaspoon of baking powder to the other flours. Use soya milk instead of dairy milk. You will need to add a little extra water to get this mixture to the right consistency. It's best to let this batter stand for about 30 minutes before using.

SPINACH AND RICOTTA

Cook 450 g/1 lb fresh spinach or 225 g/8 oz frozen leaf spinach. Drain well, really pressing out the liquid, then mix with 15 g/½ oz butter, 50 g/2 oz ricotta cheese, salt, pepper and grated nutmeg.

SWEETCORN AND CREAM CHEESE

Defrost 100 g/4 oz frozen sweetcorn kernels by putting them into a sieve and pouring boiling water over them. Put them into a bowl with 100 g/4 oz cream cheese or low-fat smooth white cheese. Mix well. Some chopped chives can be added.

AVOCADO AND TABASCO

Peel, stone and dice 1 ripe avocado. Sprinkle with lemon juice, salt, pepper and tabasco. A little crushed garlic, or some chopped chives can be added.

CAMEMBERT AND PINE NUTS

Dice 225 g/8 oz Camembert cheese and mix with 50 g/2 oz lightly toasted pine nuts.

RED PEPPER, TOMATO AND CHILLI

Grill then skin 1 large red pepper and, if you like the heat, ½ fresh red chilli (seeds removed). Chop and mix with a large skinned, seeded and chopped tomato. Season with salt and pepper.

COURGETTE AND TOMATO

Fry 1 small chopped onion in 1 tablespoon of oil for 10 minutes, then add 225 g/8 oz diced courgettes and 2 skinned, seeded and chopped tomatoes, and cook for about 5 minutes, or until the courgette is just tender. Add 1 tablespoon finely chopped parsley and some salt and pepper.

CREAMY MUSHROOM

Fry 100 g/4 oz washed and sliced button mushrooms in 15 g/½ oz butter for 15–20 minutes, or until all the liquid which they produce has boiled away. Then stir in ½ teaspoon cornflour and 100 ml/4 fl oz single cream. Stir well for about 2 minutes, until thickened, then remove from the heat. Season with salt and pepper, grated nutmeg and a squeeze of lemon juice.

TO FINISH THE DISH

Carefully arrange a good tablespoonful of the chosen mixture in the centre of each pancake and fold over the edges to make a parcel. Put this, seam side down, in a shallow gratin dish, packing in all the 'parcels' in a single layer. If you really want to play up the parcel idea you could even tie them with a long chive. They can be topped with 4–6 tablespoons of cream, or sprinkled with some grated Parmesan or, for vegans, fine breadcrumbs and dots of margarine.

Put them into a moderate oven preset to 180°C/ 350°F/Gas Mark 4 and bake for 20 minutes, just to heat them through.

Serve with a fresh Tomato Sauce (page 22) and cooked green beans or buttered broccoli; or a shredded lettuce or lettuce heart salad. Creamy mashed potatoes go well, too, if you want to make this a more substantial meal.

OPPOSITE: *Santa's Surprise Parcels*

LUNCHES, SUPPERS AND SNACKS

43

CHESTNUT–STUFFED MUSHROOMS

I think these big, juicy mushrooms with their chestnut topping make a lovely festive dish. For extra crunch, I have arranged the mushrooms on crisp croûtes — but these are optional and can be omitted if you prefer. You can use either fresh chestnuts, vacuum-packed ones or, as a last resort, canned whole chestnuts. You will need about 450 g/1 lb fresh chestnuts to give the quantity used below.

8 large open mushrooms	fresh lemon juice
olive oil for frying	salt and freshly ground
	black pepper
FOR THE STUFFING	grated nutmeg
25 g/1 oz butter or vegan	
margarine	FOR THE CROÛTES
1 large onion, finely	8 slices of wholewheat
chopped	bread
350 g/12 oz whole	about 50 g/2 oz soft
cooked chestnuts	butter

If you're making the croûtes, it's a good idea to get them done in advance and out of the way. You can fry them, but I think they're much nicer baked to a crisp golden crunchiness in a slow oven. Set the oven to 150°C/300°F/Gas Mark 2. Stamp circles in the bread with a large pastry cutter; spread on both sides with butter and put them on a baking sheet. Bake for 1 hour, or until completely crisp and golden. Cool. These will keep in a tin for a few days.

To prepare the mushrooms, cut off any stalks so that the surface is level, then wash the mushrooms and pat them dry on kitchen paper. Fry them on both sides in the olive oil and drain well. Season them with salt and pepper, then leave on one side while you make the stuffing.

Melt the butter in a medium-large saucepan. Add the onion and fry for about 7 minutes, until soft. Chop up any pieces of mushroom stalk, add these and cook for a minute or two longer. Remove from the heat and add the cooked chestnuts, breaking them up

a bit as you do so to make a mixture which holds together but has some chunky bits in it. Add a dash of fresh lemon juice, and salt, pepper and grated nutmeg to taste.

To serve the dish, preset the oven to 200°C/400°F/Gas Mark 6, or preheat the grill to high. Put the croûtes on a baking sheet or in a shallow casserole, then place a mushroom on each one, black side up. Spoon the stuffing mixture on top. Bake or grill until heated through — about 10 minutes under the grill, 15–20 minutes in the oven.
SERVES 4

FESTIVE RED CABBAGE

This is a useful dish because it cooks slowly and won't spoil if you cook it too long or keep it waiting! It also adds a moistness to the meal which often avoids the need for a separate sauce — and it's delicious, especially if you reheat it the next day.

900 g/2 lb red cabbage	150 ml/5 fl oz vegetable
50 g/2 oz butter or vegan	stock or water
margarine	salt and freshly ground
2 large onions, sliced	black pepper
150 ml/5 fl oz red wine	dash of sugar
	2–4 garlic cloves, crushed

Shred the cabbage, discarding the tough core. Melt half the butter in a large saucepan or casserole and fry the onions for about 5 minutes; then put in the cabbage and stir well, to coat it thoroughly with the butter.

Pour in the wine and stock, and add a teaspoonful of salt. Bring to the boil, then either cover, turn the heat right down and cook for about 1 hour on top of the stove, or cover and cook in an oven preset to 170°C/325°F/Gas Mark 3 for about 1½ hours. The cabbage should be very tender.

Mix the rest of the butter with the crushed garlic and add to the cabbage, along with salt, pepper and a dash of sugar to taste.
SERVES 4–6

OPPOSITE: *(right) Festive Red Cabbage and (left) Chestnut-Stuffed Mushrooms*

Try a Nordic version of this cabbage, too: add chopped apples and spices and take out the garlic.

TAGLIATELLE WITH CREAMY WALNUT SAUCE

This is a lovely pasta dish to make at Christmas when there are good walnuts around. Get some help on cracking them – or use really fresh shelled ones.

1 tbls olive oil
450 g/1 lb tagliatelle or
  fettucine
15 g/½ oz butter

FOR THE SAUCE
225 g/8 oz walnuts in
  their shells, or 100–125 g/
  4–5 oz shelled walnuts

1 garlic clove, peeled
150 ml/5 fl oz whipping
  cream
salt and freshly ground
  black pepper
freshly grated Parmesan
  cheese (optional)

To make the pasta, fill a large saucepan two-thirds full of water, add the oil, and bring to the boil.

Meanwhile, grind the walnuts and garlic in a food processor and gradually add the cream and some salt and pepper.

When the water boils, add the pasta, give it a quick stir, then leave to cook for about 6 minutes, or according to instructions on the packet. Don't let it get soggy! As soon as it's just done, drain it gently, add the butter and some salt and pepper, stirring very gently with a fork.

Add the sauce, mix quickly and lightly, and serve immediately, on warmed plates. Serve Parmesan cheese separately for those who want it; it's best grated straight on to the hot pasta.
SERVES 4

SANTA'S SACKS

Many other ingredients could be used with the potatoes for the filling here instead of sweetcorn and peanuts – I've used this combination because it's unfailingly popular with the kids I know. A can of chick peas, well drained, is good instead of sweetcorn, or chopped fried mushrooms, cheese or chopped nuts.

1 × 375 g/12 oz packet of
  filo pastry
4–6 tbls olive oil

FOR THE FILLING
1 onion, chopped
1 tbls olive oil

350 g/12 oz potatoes
50 g/2 oz frozen
  sweetcorn kernels
50 g/2 oz salted peanuts
salt and freshly ground
  pepper

First make the filling. In a medium-sized saucepan, fry the onion gently in the oil, with a lid on the pan, for 5 minutes. Meanwhile, cut the potatoes into small dice, add these to the onions, give them a stir, then cover and cook for 5 minutes. After that, put in 4 tablespoons of water, stir and cover, and continue to let them cook until the potatoes are tender – about another 5–10 minutes. Take the pan off the heat and stir in the sweetcorn, peanuts and seasoning to taste.

Set the oven to 200°C/400°F/Gas Mark 6. To make the sacks, take a piece of filo pastry and cut it into two squares about 15 cm/6 inches square. (Keep the rest covered with polythene or a damp cloth to prevent it from drying out.) Brush one of the squares with oil, then put the second one on top and brush with oil again. Put a good spoonful of the filling mixture into the centre, then dampen the edges with water and draw them up together, to make a sack. Brush the outside of the sack all over with more oil and put it on to a baking sheet. Continue like this until you have used up all the filling. (Any filo pastry which is left over can be put back in its wrappings – the packet will keep well in the fridge for at least a month if it's well sealed.)

Bake the sacks for about 20 minutes, or until they are crisp and golden all over, then serve at once.
MAKES 8

OPPOSITE: *Tagliatelle with Creamy Walnut Sauce*

OYSTER MUSHROOM RISOTTO

This makes a soothing and welcome meal at Christmas. It's easy to make and needs only a simple salad — sliced lettuce hearts, or tomatoes, for instance — to accompany it.

75 g/3 oz butter
1 large onion, chopped
1 garlic clove, crushed
300 g/10 oz arborio rice
150 ml/5 fl oz white
  wine — or use extra
  water

1 l/1¾ pints water or
  stock
100 g/4 oz oyster
  mushrooms
grated Parmesan cheese,
  to serve

Melt 50 g/2 oz of the butter in a large saucepan, add the onion and garlic and fry for 10 minutes, without browning. Put in the rice, some salt and the wine, then gradually add the water, mixing after each addition (it should moisten the rice each time) and bring to the boil. The mixture should cook for about 20 minutes in all.

Melt the remaining butter, stir in the oyster mushrooms, and add these, too, to the mixture. Bring back to a simmer, then leave the rice to cook for a further 15 minutes, stirring it often as the liquid is absorbed, to prevent it from sticking. The risotto is done when it is creamy in consistency, without any excess liquid, and the rice is tender. If the liquid is absorbed before the rice is quite done, either put a lid on the pan and leave it off the heat for 10–15 minutes, or add a little more liquid and continue to simmer it gently for a few more minutes. Season with salt and freshly ground black pepper. Serve with the grated Parmesan cheese.

SERVES 2–3 AS MAIN COURSE

FATHER CHRISTMAS FACES

These can be made on lots of different bases, but here I have used soft white or brown salad rolls, which are about 10 cm/4 inches across — just right. Cut them in half and toast them, then cover the entire surface with home-made tomato sauce, or very finely chopped seeded tomato seasoned with salt and pepper. Then put a layer of grated Italian Mozzarella cheese around the top to make hair and fur, and around the base to make a beard (you'll need about 100 g/4 oz cheese).

Cut almost-halves of small black olives and position for shiny eyes, a piece of red pepper, cut curvy, for the mouth, and a round of it for the nose and a final slice or two above the cheese for his hat. Make some of the cheese into eyebrows.

Grill just to heat through — not too much or the cheese will melt too much and brown, and the effect will be lost. (If you don't have any Mozzarella, other white cheese, such as Wensleydale or Lancashire could be used, coarsely grated.)

OPPOSITE: *Father Christmas Faces*

FLAKY MUSHROOM CHRISTMAS TREE

350 g/12 oz Quick Flaky Pastry (page 29)	*450 g/1 lb mushrooms, sliced*
egg yolk	*75 g/3 oz cooked rice*
	75 g/3 oz cream cheese
FOR THE FILLING	*1 tbls chopped parsley*
25 g/1 oz butter	*1 tsp grated lemon rind*
1 onion, sliced	*2–3 tsp lemon juice*
1 garlic clove, crushed	*salt and freshly ground black pepper*

To make the filling, melt the butter in a small saucepan. Add the onion and cook for 5 minutes, then add the garlic and mushrooms. Fry until the mushrooms are tender and any liquid which they produce has gone – this can take 30 minutes. Add the rice, cream cheese, parsley, lemon rind and juice, and salt and pepper, stirring to mix well. Chill.

Set the oven to 200°C/400°F/Gas Mark 6. On a lightly floured board, roll out the pastry into a rectangle 30 cm/12 inches long by 40 cm/16 inches wide. Cut in half to give two rectangles of 30 cm/12 inches by 20 cm/8 inches. Cut each of these into a Christmas tree as indicated on the diagram below – or better if you can! Put one of the 'trees' on to a damp baking sheet. Spoon the filling on top, leaving a little gap – not more than 1 cm/½ inch – around the edges. Dampen the edges, then put the second tree on top, pressing the edges together to seal. Prick

lightly, then decorate with little cut-out pastry shapes, stuck on with cold water: a tiny angel or a star on the top, more little stars, hearts, teddy bears, crescents crackers, or whatever, all over. You can also write HAPPY XMAS diagonally across it, if you have the patience to cut the letters! Brush with egg yolk, salt and water and bake for 30 minutes, or until the pastry is nicely browned.

Serve piping hot, with the sauce.

SERVES 4–6

CREAM AND HERB SAUCE

150 ml/5 fl oz double cream	*1 tbls chopped fresh herbs – parsley, chives, tarragon*
1 tbls lemon juice	
salt and freshly ground pepper	

Put the cream and lemon juice into a small pan and stir gently until hot. Add the seasoning and herbs, and serve.

KATE'S BUTTERBEAN CROQUETTES

My daughter Kate invented this dish, which is very simple to make and very popular with the kids. It's very quick to whizz up too – but it also freezes well. You can add extra spices, such as a teaspoonful of cumin seeds and ground coriander, fried with onion; or a dash of tomato chutney or chopped parsley, mixed in with the beans. They're good hot with Cranberry Sauce (page 23) or mango chutney; or cold, with yogurt and fresh herbs.

2 tsp olive oil	*salt and freshly ground black pepper*
1 onion, chopped	
2 × 425 g/15 oz cans butterbeans	*dried wholewheat breadcrumbs*
	olive oil for baking

Heat the oil in a large saucepan, add the onion and fry, with a lid on the pan, for about 10 minutes, or until it is tender and lightly browned. Remove the pan from the heat. Drain the butterbeans (you won't need the liquid) and add them to the pan, mashing them with a spoon or with a potato masher to make a lumpy mixture which holds together. Season with salt and pepper as necessary.

Divide the mixture into eight pieces, form into croquette shapes and coat in dried wholewheat breadcrumbs. Arrange them on a greased baking sheet. When you're ready to bake the croquettes, put them into an oven preset to 200°C/400°F/Gas Mark 6 and bake them for about 30 minutes, or until they are brown and crisp on the outside, turning them over after about 20 minutes.

MAKES 8 CROQUETTES, SERVING 4

AVOCADO WITH CURRIED BRAZILNUT STUFFING

These hot avocados make a good quick lunch or supper. They are quite rich, so go well with something plain and low in fat – like brown rice cooked so that it's nice and fluffy, with a few fresh herbs added.

2 large ripe avocados	100 g/4 oz brazilnuts,
juice of 1 lemon	chopped
6–8 spring onions	salt and freshly ground
1 tbls olive oil	pepper
2 tsp curry powder	chilli powder

Halve the avocados and remove the stones. Using a teaspoon, scoop out the flesh without damaging the skin. Cut the flesh into rough chunks, put them into a bowl and add enough lemon juice to coat the pieces.

Next, wash and trim the spring onions, then slice finely. Heat the oil in a medium saucepan, add the onions and curry powder and fry over a gentle heat for 4–5 minutes, or until the spring onions are tender. Remove from the heat and add the avocado, chopped brazilnuts, salt and pepper to taste, and a pinch or two of chilli to give it as much kick as you wish.

Heat the grill. Stand the avocado skins on a grill pan or flameproof dish, spoon the brazilnut mixture into the skins and grill for 5–10 minutes, or until the filling is heated through and the top is lightly browned.
SERVES 4

SHOPPER'S DELIGHT

¼ iceberg lettuce	100 g/4 oz green pepper,
4 wholewheat pitta	sliced
breads	
2 tsp olive oil	FOR THE GARLIC SAUCE
100 g/4 oz leek, finely	150 ml/5 fl oz soured
sliced	cream or Greek yogurt
100 g/4 oz cabbage,	1–2 garlic cloves, crushed
finely shredded	salt and freshly ground
100 g/4 oz button	pepper
mushrooms, sliced	

First make the garlic sauce by putting the soured cream or yogurt into a small saucepan with the garlic and seasoning with salt and pepper to taste. Leave on one side.

Finely shred the lettuce, and keep that on one side, too. Halve the pitta breads through the middle so that each one makes two pockets. Put these under the grill to warm through, but don't toast them.

Meanwhile, heat the oil in a large saucepan, add the leek, cabbage, mushrooms and green pepper and stir-fry for about 2 minutes, or until heated through. Gently heat the soured cream or yogurt and garlic, without letting it get anywhere near boiling.

Now fill the pitta pockets: put in a spoonful of shredded lettuce, then plenty of the stir-fried vegetables. Top with a good spoonful of the warm garlic sauce and finish with some more lettuce. Eat at once.
SERVES 4

CHRISTMAS EVE
COUSCOUS

FOR THE VEGETABLE
 STEW
50 g/2 oz butter
450 g/1 lb onions, sliced
450 g/1 lb carrots, sliced
700 g/1½ lb acorn
 squash, peeled, seeded
 and diced
1 tsp ground ginger
½ tsp powdered cinnamon
½ tsp turmeric
¼–½ tsp ground white
 pepper
900 ml/1½ pints water or
 vegetable stock
450 g/1 lb courgettes,
 trimmed and sliced
450 g/1 lb frozen broad
 beans (or sweetcorn)
salt

squeeze of lemon juice
dash of sugar
chopped fresh coriander

FOR THE GRAIN
450 g/1 lb couscous
1 tsp salt
50 g/2 oz butter

FOR THE EXTRAS
1 tbls harissa sauce
1 × 425 g/15 oz can chick
 peas, drained
1 tbls olive oil
1 tsp cumin seeds
125–175 g/5–6 oz
 raisins
100 g/4 oz pine nuts
225 g/8 oz Greek yogurt
a dusting of paprika

First make the stew. Melt the butter in a large saucepan. Add the onions and fry for 5 minutes, then add the carrots, squash and spices. Cook for a further 10 minutes, with a lid on, stirring from time until all are buttery and spicy. Add the water or stock and simmer for 10–15 minutes, or until the vegetables are just becoming tender. Add the courgettes and broad beans, and cook for a further 5 minutes or so. Season with salt, lemon juice, and a little sugar if necessary. (This is best made in advance and reheated, as the flavours improve – it is particularly good after freezing.)

Now make the grain. This is an unusual way to cook couscous, but I find it gives the best results. Put the couscous into a baking tin and add 600 ml/1 pint of water; immediately drain this off and return the couscous to the tin. Leave it for 20 minutes, separating the grains with your fingers after 10 minutes, or more times if you're passing. Put the couscous into a sieve or steamer lined with a blue J-cloth. Set over a pan of simmering water (it doesn't

have to be the stew) for 20 minutes. Tip the couscous back into the baking tin, and pour over 150 ml/5 fl oz cold water with the salt dissolved in it. Sift the grains with your fingers and leave for 15 minutes, then put back into the lined steamer and heat as above for a further 20 minutes. Sift with your fingers into a serving bowl and stir in the butter. Set aside while you put together the extras.

To assemble and serve, take a ladleful of liquid from the stew and add it to the harissa to make a thick paste. Put this into a small bowl. Drain the chick peas. In a small pan, heat the oil and add the cumin seeds, stirring for a moment or two, then add the chick peas and stir until heated through. Put into a second small bowl. Cover the raisins with boiling water, leave for 10 minutes or longer to plump, then drain and put into a third small bowl. Put the pine nuts into a fourth bowl – they can be lightly toasted if you like. Finally, put the yogurt into a fifth bowl and dust the top with some paprika.

To serve, ladle the stew over the couscous and garnish with chopped fresh coriander.
SERVES 6

OPPOSITE: *Christmas Eve Couscous*

PARTIES AND BUFFETS

Christmas 'parties' cover a whole host of different occasions, ranging from a few simple nibbles with drinks to a full-blown buffet-style meal. This chapter, therefore, includes a variety of recipes to enable you to cope with *all* the very different festive entertaining you are likely to do. There are simple dips and savouries, as well as more substantial 'centrepiece' dishes and salads, along with some festive drinks, some with alcohol, some without. I hope you'll find something here to fit your particular needs – and don't forget to check other, appropriate chapters, too: light savouries in Lunches, Suppers and Snacks (pages 30 to 53), which are good for drinks parties, for instance, while some of the main courses in Christmas Dinners (pages 76 to 103), could make very effective dishes for a buffet or fork supper.

One of the main problems when catering for a party is to know how much food to make. I generally go right back to basics and think in terms of individual portions – how much any one person would reasonably eat. For a drinks party, I think about five or six little savouries per person is about right, and it's nice if some of these are hot and some cold. Quite a few of the recipes I've given here can be made in advance and frozen, then cooked or heated and served with dips, crudités, crisps and small savoury biscuits, for a relaxed, hassle-free occasion. Along with the food, allow about half a bottle of wine per person, or the equivalent in other drinks, plus some non-alcoholic drinks as well. Mulled Wine (page 75) is a particularly welcoming drink for a Christmas or New Year Party, although you should probably plan on serving wine at ordinary temperatures, too.

A buffet or fork supper can be as simple or as elaborate as you want to make it. You could serve just one really delicious main course with a salad, bread, cheeses and a pudding; usually, though, I think it's best to serve a choice of at least two main courses (most people will have a little of each, so allow for this when you calculate quantities), plus three or four salads and/or vegetables, of which people will have only a spoonful or so. One golden rule, when estimating amounts I've found, is that a group of people never, for some reason, eat as much salad as they would at a smaller gathering. Again, if you think in terms of what one person would eat and multiply up by the number of your guests, you'll be on roughly the right track.

I haven't given separate pudding recipes in this chapter, although no real buffet is complete without one or two. There is, however, a whole range of spectacular and suitable offerings in Festive Puddings (pages 104 to 123). Perhaps the best idea is to choose two to finish your party in style, one that is rich (the Chocolate Charlotte with Chocolate Holly Leaves, page 110 or Buche de Noel, page 132 would fit the bill nicely), and one that is refreshing (like Rum-Marinated Fruits with Coconut and Lime Cream, page 116 or Christmas Dried Fruit Salad, page 112).

RED PEPPER AND GARLIC DIP

2 large red peppers
6 large garlic cloves, peeled
150 ml/5 fl oz light olive oil
1–2 tbls lemon juice

salt and freshly ground black pepper
25–50 g/1–2 oz soft white breadcrumbs (optional)

Quarter the peppers, removing the stems and seeds, then put into a saucepan with the garlic and water just to cover. Bring to the boil, then simmer for about 15 minutes, or until the peppers are very tender. Drain well and leave until cold.

Put the peppers and garlic into a food processor and purée, gradually adding the oil and lemon juice to make a soft, creamy mixture like mayonnaise. Season, then chill before serving.

The dip will thicken slightly as it stands, but if you wish you can thicken it a bit more by stirring in some breadcrumbs. Add these gradually, allowing them several minutes to swell and thicken the mixture before adding more.

SERVES 6–8 AS A FIRST COURSE

HUMMUS

This is a useful dip to have at Christmas, or almost any time, and makes a good creamy vegan salad dressing, too. Be sure to get the deliciously mild pale golden-beige tahini, not the dark brown one. It keeps for ages.

1 × 425 g/15 oz can chick peas
1 garlic clove, peeled
2 tbls tahini
5 tbls olive oil

juice of 1 lemon
salt and freshly ground black pepper
extra olive oil and paprika, to serve

Drain the chick peas, keeping the liquid. Put the chick peas into a food processor with the garlic and whizz

to a thick purée, scraping down the sides as necessary. Add the tahini, oil, a tablespoonful of the lemon juice and a little of the reserved chick pea liquid, and whizz again. Keep on adding the reserved liquid until you have a smooth, creamy consistency, like lightly whipped cream. Taste the mixture and add more lemon juice if necessary then season with salt and pepper.

To serve, spoon the hummus into a bowl, swirl a little olive oil on top and sprinkle with paprika.

SERVES 4 AS A FIRST COURSE

AVOCADO DIP

Just about everyone's favourite, this is very easy to whizz up, and makes a lovely dressing for salad, too.

1 large ripe avocado
1 tomato
1 small green chilli (optional)

1–2 garlic cloves
juice of 1 lime or lemon
salt and freshly ground pepper

Halve the avocado, then remove the stone and peel. Mash the flesh roughly with a fork, or whizz it in a food processor if you want a thinner, creamier texture. Peel, seed and chop the tomato and add to the mixture.

Wash, seed and finely chop the chilli, if you're using this, and add it to the avocado, being careful to wash your hands afterwards; then add the garlic and enough lime or lemon juice to give the dip a good tang. Season with salt and pepper and serve as soon as possible.

This dip looks nice garnished with a leaf or two of fresh coriander or flatleaf parsley, a sprinkling of paprika pepper or a thin slice of lime or lemon.

SERVES 4–6

OPPOSITE: *A selection of party dips (from left to right) Avocado, Red Pepper and Garlic, Hummus and Smoky Aubergine (page 58)*

SMOKY AUBERGINE DIP

Any of the dips on page 56 and here would make good toppings for Crostini.

3 medium aubergines	salt and freshly ground
1 garlic clove, peeled	black pepper
3 tbls olive oil	2–3 tsp red wine vinegar
juice of 1–2 lemons	chopped fresh parsley
	black olives

Cut the aubergines in half and place them, cut side down, under a hot grill for about 20 minutes until the skin is charred and the flesh feels soft. Leave them to cool, then remove the skin – it comes off very easily.

Put the flesh into a processor with the garlic, oil and a couple of tablespoons of lemon juice, and whizz to a smooth, creamy purée. Taste and season, adding more lemon juice and the red wine vinegar as necessary, to give a good piquant flavour.

Spoon the mixture into a small bowl, and serve sprinkled with chopped fresh parsley and garnished with some black olives.

SERVES 4

MASCARPONE AND HERB DIP

A rich and creamy dip for a party. You could make a less rich version by using curd cheese or, even less calorific, a skimmed milk smooth white cheese. Serve surrounded by crudités: radishes, baby sweetcorn, celery sticks, cauliflower florets, etc.

250 g/9 oz mascarpone	1–2 tbls chopped parsley
3–4 tbls plain yogurt	tabasco
2 garlic cloves, crushed	salt and freshly ground
1 tsp grated onion	pepper
1–2 tbls chopped chives	

Put the mascarpone into a bowl, add the yogurt, garlic and onion, and beat until creamy. Add the chives, parsley, a few drops of tabasco to taste, and some salt and pepper. Chill until needed.

SERVES 10

ASSORTED CROSTINI

These delicious crisp croûtons, with their colourful toppings, are very useful for parties. In keeping with the occasion, they can be hearty, in true Tuscan style, or delicate, depending on the size of the croûton bases.

A fairly slim French stick, sliced into rounds a bit less than 1 cm/½ inch thick, makes a good, average-size crostini; or, for mini ones, you can use bridge rolls, similarly sliced, to make smaller rounds. Put the rounds on baking sheets and put them in a coolish oven – 150–160°C/275–300°F/Gas Mark 1–2 – for about 20–30 minutes, or until they are dry and crisp. Half way through this process, brush on both sides with olive oil, then put back into the oven to finish crisping. Let them cool on the tins.

For the toppings, you can use black olive pâté; a smooth soft goat's cheese and Tartex Swiss pâté, garnished with small sprigs of fresh herbs; pine nuts, capers, small pieces of grilled red pepper, or olives.

They're best assembled as near as possible to the time you're going to eat them so that the base remains crisp, but all the different parts, including the garnishes, can be prepared in advance.

GOAT'S CHEESE BALLS

450 g/1 lb soft medium-	2 tbls finely grated
fat goat's cheese	hazelnuts or roasted
2 tbls finely chopped	cashew nuts
chives	1–2 tbls paprika

Have three plates, one each for the chives, nuts and paprika. Break off small pieces of cheese – about the size of a marble – and divide them among the three plates. Roll them to coat the outside and form a smooth ball.

Chill, then serve piled up on a small plate.

MAKES ABOUT 15 BALLS

OPPOSITE: *Goat's Cheese Balls*

RED AND GREEN PEPPERS

3 large juicy red peppers
3 large juicy green
  peppers
juice of 1 lemon

4 tbls olive oil
salt and freshly ground
  black pepper
chopped fresh parsley

Cut the peppers into quarters, down from the stems. Place them, skin side up, under a very hot grill for about 15–20 minutes until the skin has blackened and blistered. As one area of the pepper gets blackened, turn them so that all the shiny skin gets done.

Remove from the grill and put them into a polythene bag, or between two plates, and leave them to get cold. Peel off the charred skins and rinse the peppers under cold water. Blot dry.

Cut the peppers into long thin pieces and put them into a shallow dish. Sprinkle them with lemon juice, oil and salt and pepper to taste. Leave them for a few hours if possible to allow the flavours to mellow and blend, giving them a stir from time to time. Check the seasoning, then sprinkle with parsley before serving.
SERVES 6–8 AS A FIRST COURSE

STUFFED BABY AUBERGINES

6 baby aubergines
1 tbls olive oil
1 medium-sized onion,
  finely chopped
1 garlic clove, crushed
2 tomatoes, skinned,
  seeded and chopped

25 g/1 oz pine nuts
1 tbls chopped parsley
salt and freshly ground
  black pepper
dash of lemon juice
pine nuts, to garnish

Cut the aubergines in half, leaving the stalks on. With a small sharp knife and a teaspoon, carefully scoop out the flesh without breaking the skin. Set the skins

OPPOSITE: (left) Red and Green Peppers and (right) Stuffed Baby Aubergines

aside. Chop the flesh. In a saucepan, heat the oil and fry the onion for 5 minutes, with a lid on the pan. Add the chopped aubergine flesh, garlic and tomatoes, cover and cook for a further 10–15 minutes, or until tender and purée-like.

Set the oven to 180°C/350°F/Gas Mark 4. Blanch the skins in boiling water for 2 minutes, drain well and place in a greased shallow ovenproof dish. Add the pine nuts, parsley and lemon juice to the aubergine mixture, season and pile into the skins. Cover and bake for 20 minutes, or until browned and cooked. Serve cold, decorated with pine nuts.
SERVES 6 AS FIRST COURSE/OR 2–3 AS A LIGHT MAIN COURSE

GRILLED MUSHROOMS WITH GARLIC HERB CHEESE

These make a pleasant warm or hot nibble for a party, or, served with a salad garnish and some good bread, as a first course. You need small mushrooms, but not the very tight button ones.

225 g/8 oz mushrooms
olive oil

1 × 145 g/5 oz Boursin
  garlic and herb cheese

Wash the mushrooms, then remove the stems by pushing them first one way and then the other – they should come out quite easily. Rub the mushrooms with a little olive oil, then place them, open-side down, on a grill pan or baking sheet.

Grill them for about 5 minutes, or until they are tender, then turn them up the other way and fill the cavity with the cheese. This can be done in advance. Just before you want to serve the mushrooms, put them under a hot grill to heat them through and melt and lightly brown the cheese.

Transfer them to a serving dish, or individual plates, and serve hot, or warm.
MAKES ABOUT 16; SERVES 3–4 AS A FIRST COURSE

BROCCOLI AND STILTON TART

The hot oil treatment of the pastry case and the preliminary cooking of the custard are tips I learned from a friend renowned for her wonderfully crisp flan bases. The contrast of the creamy custard and the crisp, light pastry is excellent.

75 g/3 oz plain white flour	FOR THE FILLING
75 g/3 oz plain wholewheat flour	225 g/8 oz broccoli florets
½ tsp salt	300 ml/10 fl oz single cream
75 g/3 oz butter	3 egg yolks
1 egg yolk	salt and freshly ground
1 tbls cold water	pepper
1½ tbls oil	100 g/4 oz blue Stilton cheese, thinly sliced

Set the oven to 200°C/400°F/Gas Mark 6.

Make the pastry by putting the flours, salt, butter and egg yolk into a food processor; whizz for a few seconds without the plunger to allow the air to get in until the mixture looks like breadcrumbs, then add the water and whizz again, briefly, until the mixture forms a ball of dough. Or make the pastry in the usual way by putting the flours and salt into a bowl, rubbing in the butter with your fingertips then adding the egg yolk and water to bind to a dough.

On a floured board, roll out the pastry as thinly as you can and press gently into a 23 cm/9 inch flan tin. Trim off the excess pastry, put a circle of greaseproof paper in the base and weigh it down with some crusts or dried beans. Bake the flan case for 7 minutes, then take out the greaseproof paper and crusts or beans and bake for a further 5–10 minutes, until the pastry base looks golden and feels set and firm to the touch. Just before you take the flan case out of the oven, heat the oil in a small saucepan until it is smoking hot. Pour this over the base of the flan case as soon as it comes out of the oven. It should sizzle and seem to 'fry' on the base of the flan. Now you can leave the flan case until you're ready to finish it.

To make the filling, bring 2.5 cm/1 inch of water to the boil in a saucepan. Put in the broccoli, cover, and boil for 2–3 minutes, or until it is just tender. Drain immediately into a colander, then put under the cold tap to cool the broccoli quickly so that it keeps its crispness and colour. Turn the broccoli on to a double layer of kitchen paper and blot dry.

Put the cream and egg yolks into a saucepan and beat together. Season with a little salt and pepper, then stir over a gentle heat for a few minutes until the mixture just begins to thicken and coats the spoon. Remove from the heat immediately. Now put the broccoli and Stilton into the flan case and pour the custard over. Put into the oven, turn the heat down to 180°C/350°F/Gas Mark 4 and bake for 30–40 minutes.

SERVES 6

VARIATIONS
Brie is very good in this tart instead of the Stilton; so is Italian Mascarpone.

CELEBRATION WILD RICE WITH LEMON MAYONNAISE SAUCE

This is a pleasing mixture of flavours and textures; the chewiness and slightly smoky taste of wild rice is enhanced by the intensely flavoured porcini mushrooms, and the delicate, buttery avocado makes a complete contrast.

225 g/8 oz wild rice	LEMON MAYONNAISE
25 g/1 oz porcini mushrooms	150 ml/5 fl oz plain yogurt
2 ripe avocados	150 ml/5 fl oz soured cream
juice of 1 lemon	
2 tbls chopped chives	4 rounded tbls good quality mayonnaise, such as Hellman's
salt and freshly ground pepper	
100 g/4 oz whole roasted cashew nuts, pine nuts or macadamia nuts	juice of 1 lemon
	salt and freshly ground black pepper

First, make the rice. Put the rice into a saucepan with its height again in cold water and bring to the boil; let it simmer for about 45 minutes, or until it is tender and some of the grains have split open. Drain and put into a bowl.

Meanwhile, wash the porcini and put them into a saucepan with water to cover. Bring to the boil, then take off the heat and leave to steep for 30 minutes. After that, simmer the porcini gently for about 15 minutes, or until they are tender and all the water has been absorbed. Add the porcini to the wild rice.

Now make the lemon mayonnaise. Mix together the yogurt, cream and mayonnaise, then stir in the lemon juice, adding it a little at a time and tasting the mixture, to get the right amount of sharpness. Season with salt and freshly ground black pepper.

Halve the avocados and remove the stones and peel, then dice the flesh. Sprinkle the avocados with the lemon juice, and add these, and any extra juice, to the wild rice, along with the chopped chives. Season to taste with salt and freshly ground black pepper. Serve at once, or cover and refrigerate for up to an hour before serving. Just before serving add the nuts.

You can prepare this salad well in advance if you wish, as long as you leave out the avocado and nuts which should be added as near serving time as possible. Serve with the lemon mayonnaise.

SERVES 8–10 AT A PARTY

GNOCCHI ALLA ROMANA WITH CHAR–GRILLED VEGETABLES

Although gnocchi alla Romana is usually served as a starter, I think it makes a delicious vegetarian main course, especially when accompanied by some grilled vegetables and perhaps some Italian tomato sauce (page 22). The gnocchi freezes excellently, either as separate cut shapes, or assembled and sprinkled with Parmesan, ready for cooking.

1 l/1¾ pints milk	*salt and freshly grated*
1 bay leaf	*black pepper*
200 g/7 oz semolina	*freshly grated nutmeg*
2 egg yolks	*50 g/2 oz freshly grated*
100 g/4 oz grated cheese	*Parmesan cheese*

Put the milk and bay leaf into a large saucepan and bring to the boil. Add the semolina gradually in a thin stream, from well above the saucepan, stirring all the time. Bring the mixture to the boil, stirring, then let it cook gently for about 15 minutes until it is very thick. Remove from the heat and beat in the egg yolks and grated cheese. Season with plenty of salt, pepper and grated nutmeg. Spread the mixture out on an oiled baking sheet to a thickness of 1 cm/½ inch or a bit less, and leave to get cold and firm.

Cut the gnocchi mixture into shapes using a sharp pastry cutter, then assemble the dish. First put any odd shapes and trimmings onto a lightly greased shallow dish (a 30 cm/12 inch round ceramic pizza plate is ideal) and top with the remaining shapes. Sprinkle generously with the Parmesan cheese, then grill until the top is golden brown and bubbling, and the inside heated through.

Serve immediately.

FOR THE CHAR-GRILLED VEGETABLES
These can be grilled before the gnocchi, as they can be served warm. Remove the outer leaves from chicory and radicchio, then cut them downwards, halving the chicory and cutting the radicchio into sixths or eighths, depending on its size. Put the vegetables under a hot grill until they are lightly charred and wilted, but still crunchy, turning them over to do both sides. Put them into a serving dish, sprinkle with salt and pepper, and pour a little olive oil over them. I like to serve them with some chunky lemon wedges.

SERVES 6

MIDWINTER VEGETABLE TERRINE WITH MUSTARD VINAIGRETTE

This makes a striking dish for a buffet party. You can use other vegetables for the filling, but they need to be of contrasting colours. I love the slightly sweet, nutty flavour of Jerusalem artichokes, which luckily I find I can eat without tiresome after-affects. I sometimes wonder whether it's fair to inflict this on visitors, though, delicious as it is, and use turnips instead! Parsnips, peppers, sweet potato, firm winter squash and courgettes would all taste and look good; leek could be substituted for spinach for the outside layer.

900 g/2 lb spinach
75 g/3 oz butter or vegan
 margarine
lemon juice
2 eggs
salt and freshly ground
 black pepper
450 g/1 lb carrots
700 g/1½ lb Jerusalem
 artichokes

FOR THE MUSTARD
 VINAIGRETTE
3 tbls Dijon mustard,
 preferably Grey Poupon
3 tbls red wine vinegar
9 tbls olive oil

Wash the spinach thoroughly in three changes of water, then put it into a large saucepan with just the water clinging to it, and cook for about 10 minutes, or until it is tender. Drain it well, squeezing it really dry with your hands, or by pressing it against the sides of a sieve. Add 25 g/1 oz of the butter, a few drops of lemon juice, 1 egg, and mix well. Season with salt and pepper. Leave this on one side while you make the other two fillings.

Scrape or scrub the carrots and cut them into small dice; peel the artichokes as thinly as you can, and dice them. too. Divide the remaining butter between two pans, then put the carrots into one and the Jerusalem artichokes into the other. Cover and let them cook very gently for about 15 minutes, or until they are both tender. If they start to stick to the pan, add a tablespoonful of water. Then mash each roughly. Separate the remaining egg, and add the yolk to the carrots and the white to the Jerusalem artichokes. Mix well, adding salt, pepper and a little lemon juice to taste.

Set the oven to 180°C/350°F/Gas Mark 4. Line a 900 g/2 lb loaf tin (a long narrow one is best) with a long strip of nonstick paper to cover the base and ends, and oil the tin. Press the spinach mixture into the base and all the way up the sides, saving enough to cover the top. Put in the carrot mixture in a smooth layer, then the artichoke mixture, and finish with the rest of the spinach.

Stand the loaf tin in a baking tin and pour in boiling water so that it comes about two thirds up the sides of the tin. Bake for 50 minutes–1 hour until the top feels firm. Let it cool, then chill it. To serve, slip a knife around the edges, turn the terrine out on to a serving dish and strip off the paper. Decorate with cut-out Jerusalem artichoke stars and carrot shapes, and serve with the mustard vinaigrette.

To make the vinaigrette, put the mustard into a bowl with the vinegar, ¼ teaspoonful of salt and a grinding of pepper, and mix well. Gradually add the oil, mixing well after each addition to make a thick, emulsified dressing. Check the seasoning and add a little more salt if necessary before serving with the terrine.

SERVES 6–8

OPPOSITE: *Midwinter Vegetable Terrine with Mustard Vinaigrette*

LITTLE BRIE AND HAZELNUT BAKES

Quick, easy and delicious! Serve them with a crisp, simple salad such as lettuce, cucumber and tomato, chicory, watercress and orange (as here), or celery and apple. They're also good with lightly cooked vegetables such as French beans, and I love them with the bitter-sweet fruity flavour of home-made Cranberry Sauce (page 23).

350 g/12 oz Brie   50 g/2 oz hazelnuts, skinned

Cut the Brie (including the rind) into 1 cm/½ inch chunky pieces and place close together in a single layer in four individual ramekins, or in a shallow ovenproof dish. Chop the hazelnuts roughly – I give them a quick whizz in the food processor – and sprinkle evenly over the top.

Place under a hot grill for about 10 minutes, until the Brie has heated through and half melted, and the nuts have toasted. Serve at once.
SERVES 3–4

CHUNKY HAZELNUT AND TOMATO TERRINE

25 g/1 oz butter or margarine
1 onion, finely chopped
100 g/4 oz button mushrooms
2 tomatoes, skinned and chopped
1 garlic clove, crushed
1 tsp basil
200 g/7 oz skinned hazelnuts
100 g/4 oz fresh breadcrumbs
1 tbls chopped parsley
75 ml/3 fl oz water or stock
2 tbls Tamari or Shoyu soy sauce
1 tbls lemon juice
salt and freshly ground pepper

OPPOSITE: *Little Brie and Hazelnut Bakes*

Set the oven to 200°C/400°F/Gas Mark 6 and line a 450 g/1 lb loaf tin with a long strip of nonstick paper to cover the base and narrow sides.

To make the terrine, melt the butter in a medium-large saucepan, then add the onion and fry for 7–8 minutes until soft but not browned; then add the mushrooms, tomatoes, garlic and basil, and fry for a further 5 minutes.

Meanwhile, chop the hazelnuts coarsely. Add these to the mixture in the saucepan, along with the fresh breadcrumbs, chopped parsley, water or stock, Tamari or Shoyu soy sauce and lemon juice.

Mix well, season with salt and pepper, spoon the mixture into the prepared tin and smooth the top level. Bake, uncovered, for about 40 minutes, or until the terrine feels firm to the touch. Leave it to cool completely in the tin, then chill.

Serve cold, thinly sliced, with warm Garlic Sauce (page 51).
SERVES 8 AT A PARTY

MUSHROOM PÂTÉ WITH A HERBY CRUST

Cold and sliced, this makes a good pâté for a party – the Lemon Mayonnaise (page 62) goes very well with this, especially if you throw a few green peppercorns into it (about a tablespoonful). This pâté also makes a good first course and is an excellent sandwich filling, especially if you use a rather light, granary bread.

25 g/1 oz butter	FOR THE HERBY
1 onion, chopped	COATING
700 g/1½ lb mushrooms	extra butter for coating
2 garlic cloves, crushed	dried wholewheat crumbs
50 g/2 oz fresh	1½ tsp mixed herbs
breadcrumbs	
1 egg	
salt and freshly ground	
pepper	

Set the oven to 180°C/350°F/Gas Mark 4 and line a greased 450 g/1 lb loaf tin with a long strip of nonstick paper to cover the base and narrow sides. Grease the paper very generously with butter, then sprinkle thickly with dried wholewheat crumbs and 1 teaspoonful of the mixed herbs, to form the herby coating.

To make the pâté, melt the butter in a large saucepan, add the onion and fry for 5 minutes; then add the mushrooms and garlic, and fry for about 30 minutes or until all the liquid has gone. Whizz the mushroom mixture to a purée in a food processor; add the breadcrumbs and egg, and whizz again briefly, to mix.

Pour the mixture into the prepared tin and smooth the top level. Sprinkle the top quite thickly with dried crumbs, sprinkle with the remaining mixed herbs and dot with a little butter. Bake, uncovered, for about 40 minutes, or until the pâté feels firm to the touch, and a knife inserted in the middle comes out clean. Leave it to cool in the tin, then loosen the sides, turn the pâté out and strip off the paper. If you want a crisper coating, pop the pâté back into the oven for 10 minutes or so, or until the outside is crisp.

Serve cold, thinly sliced.

SERVES 8 AT A PARTY

MINI CHESTNUT SAUSAGE ROLLS

These little 'sausages' are very popular with children. They freeze excellently, too, and can be baked from frozen – allow 5 minutes extra cooking time if you are doing this. They are good served with a dip, such as yogurt and herb, soured cream and horseradish, or with mango chutney.

225 g/8 oz quick flaky	1 garlic clove, crushed
pastry (page 29)	1 tbls lemon juice
	1 tbls soy sauce
FOR THE FILLING	100 g/4 oz soft
1 × 250 g/8 oz can	wholewheat breadcrumbs
unsweetened chestnut	good pinch of chilli
purée	powder
1 small onion, grated	flour for rolling

First make the chestnut filling, by mixing together the chestnut purée, onion, garlic, lemon juice, soy sauce, breadcrumbs and chilli powder. Leave the mixture for a few minutes for the breadcrumbs to thicken it, then add a few more if necessary to make a soft mixture which you can roll into sausages.

Set the oven to 190°C/375°F/Gas Mark 5.

On a lightly floured board, roll out the pastry quite thinly, then cut across into long strips about 5 cm/2 inches wide. Roll pieces of the chestnut mixture into sausages about the width of a slim little finger and the length of the pastry strips, and lay on top of the pastry strips. Dampen the edges of the pastry with cold water, then roll them round the chestnut mixture, pressing the edges together. Prick the pastry with a fork, then cut into 2.5 cm/1 inch lengths and place, seam side down, on a baking sheet. Bake for about 10 minutes, or until the pastry is golden brown and crisp.

MAKES 48

OPPOSITE: *Mini Chestnut Sausage Rolls*

PARTY ROULADE

FOR THE ROULADE
*50 g/2 oz soft white
breadcrumbs*
*150 ml/5 fl oz single
cream*
2 tbls water
*175 g/6 oz Gruyère
cheese, grated*
4 eggs, separated
*salt and freshly ground
black pepper*
cayenne pepper

*a little grated Parmesan
for dusting*

FOR THE FILLING
450 g/1 lb asparagus
2 tbls lemon juice
2 tbls olive oil
*150 g/5 oz Lingot du
Berry or other, similar
soft medium fat goat's
cheese*
1 tbls chopped parsley

Set the oven to 200°C/400°F/Gas Mark 6 and line a
32 × 23 cm/13 × 9 inch Swiss roll tin with nonstick
paper.

First make the roulade. Mix together the breadcrumbs, cream, water, cheese and egg yolks. Season
with salt, pepper and a couple of pinches of cayenne.

Whisk the egg whites until stiff, then fold into the
egg yolk mixture. Turn into a tin, spreading into the
corners – get it level. Bake for 10–15 minutes or until
set and firm to a light touch. Level it in the tin and
cover it with a tea towel which has been rung out in
warm water. Set it aside to get completely cold.

To make the filling, trim and cook the asparagus
until just tender; drain. Cut off the tips and chop the
rest. Put it all into a shallow dish, sprinkle with the
lemon juice, oil and season. Leave to get cold.

To assemble the roulade, sprinkle a large sheet of
nonstick paper with grated Parmesan. Remove the
cloth from the roulade and turn the roulade out on to
the paper. Trim the edges. Spread the goat's cheese
all over the roulade. Remove 8 tips from the
asparagus and put the rest over the roulade, on top of
the cheese (don't use the dressing which may remain
with the asparagus). Sprinkle with the parsley.

Carefully roll up the roulade, using the paper to
help. Place on a dish and decorate with the reserved
asparagus tips, placed diagonally along the top.
SERVES 6

MIXED LEAF SALAD WITH ROCKET

This is a mixture of radiccio, frisée, lamb's lettuce,
some ordinary 'floppy' lettuce – not too much! –
rocket (which you can sometimes get growing in a
pot) and some freshly chopped herbs if available,
especially tarragon and chives. I usually serve with a
'normal' vinaigrette, which I generally make with 1
tablespoon wine vinegar to 3 tablespoons olive oil, a
good pinch of sugar, about half a teaspoon Dijon
mustard, preferably Grey Poupon, and some sea salt
and pepper. Tear up the leaves, making sure there's a
nice mix of colours, with plenty of red.

CUCUMBER AND DILL SALAD

1 large cucumber
1 small onion (optional)
*salt, sugar and freshly
ground pepper*

1 tsp white mustard seed
*1 tbls chopped fresh dill
or 1 tsp dried dill weed*
2 tbls wine vinegar

Peel and thinly slice the cucumber and the onion, if
you're using this. Put the slices into a shallow dish
and sprinkle with a little salt, pepper and a dash of
sugar (about ½ teaspoonful). Mix in the mustard seed,
dill and vinegar, cover and leave until you need it.

The salad will make quite a lot of juice – that's
normal. Drain it off before serving, or not, as you
wish. It's nice mopped up with some bread.
SERVES 4

OPPOSITE: *Party Roulade*

LETTUCE HEART SALAD WITH FRESH HERB DRESSING

2 hearty lettuces, such as little gem
1 tbls chopped fresh herbs — tarragon is especially good if you can get it; otherwise chives or mint
½ tsp Dijon mustard
good pinch of sugar
salt and freshly ground black pepper
1 tbls red wine vinegar
3 tbls olive oil

Wash the lettuces, taking off the outer leaves but keeping the hearts intact; then slice. Put the herbs, mustard, sugar, some salt and pepper and the vinegar into a salad bowl — a glass one is nice — and mix together. Gradually stir in the oil. Cross salad servers over the top of the dressing and put the lettuce in on top. Gently toss the lettuce in the dressing just before you serve the salad.
SERVES 3–4

CHICORY, ORANGE AND WATERCRESS SALAD

The juice from the oranges provides a light dressing for this refreshing salad, although you can add 1–2 tablespoons of olive oil to make it into more of a vinaigrette-type of dressing if you prefer. Ruby oranges are particularly good if you can get them.

2 chicory
4 small sweet oranges
1 × 75 g/3 oz packet of watercress

Wash the chicory and cut it downwards into eighths and put it into a bowl. Holding the oranges over the bowl to catch the juice, cut the peel and pith, then slice them into thin circles. Add the watercress and toss all the ingredients together.
SERVES 4

COLESLAW

Coleslaw is so quick and easy to make, and the home-made version so good, that I wonder why people buy it ready-made . . .

450 g/1 lb white cabbage, finely shredded
225 g/8 oz scraped carrots, coarsely grated
150 ml/5 fl oz low fat plain yogurt
4 tbls mayonnaise
salt and freshly ground pepper
lemon juice (optional)

OPTIONAL ADDITIONS
2 onions, finely sliced
1 small green pepper, seeded and chopped
100 g/4 oz raisins

Put the cabbage and carrots into a large bowl, together with any of the optional extras. Add the yogurt, mayonnaise and salt and pepper to taste and mix well. Sharpen with a little lemon juice if you like, before serving.
SERVES 6

WATERCRESS AND RADISH SALAD

This is an easy salad to make — and a pretty, festive combination of colours, too. It tastes wonderfully fresh as is, but if you prefer, you can serve dressed with a light vinaigrette.

1 × 100 g/4 oz packet radishes
1 × 75 g/3 oz packet watercress

Wash the radishes, and halve them or leave them whole, as you wish. Give the watercress a quick swish through cold water, then shake dry and put into a bowl with the radishes.
SERVES 4

OPPOSITE: *(left) Broccoli and Stilton Tart, page 62, and (right) Lettuce Heart Salad with Fresh Herb Dressing*

MELON AND STAR FRUIT COMPÔTE

A melon with greenish flesh looks good with the yellow star fruit – either an ogen melon, or a honeydew, for instance. These are best bought a few days before you need them, so that they can ripen up. I choose the yellowest star fruit that I can find.

1 ripe melon	clear honey
juice of 2 oranges	1 large ripe star fruit

Halve the melon, remove the seeds, then cut the flesh into pieces or scoop it out with a parisienne cutter to make melon balls. Put the melon into a bowl with the orange juice and a little honey to taste, as necessary. If the melon is sweet you probably won't need any honey.

Just before you want to serve the compôte, cut the star fruit across – like slicing a cucumber – to produce thin star-shaped pieces. Add to the compôte, then divide the mixture between six bowls.

CASHEW NUT ROAST WITH HERB STUFFING

50 g/2 oz butter	FOR THE STUFFING
1 large onion, sliced	100 g/4 oz white
225 g/8 oz unroasted	breadcrumbs
cashew nuts	50 g/2 oz butter
100 g/4 oz white bread,	1 small onion, grated
crusts removed	$\frac{1}{2}$ tsp each thyme and
2 large garlic cloves	marjoram
200 ml/7 fl oz water or	25 g/1 oz parsley,
light vegetable stock	chopped
salt and freshly ground	parsley sprigs and small
black pepper	lemon slices, to garnish
grated nutmeg	
1 tbls lemon juice	

Set the oven to 200°C/400°F/Gas Mark 6 and line a 450 g/1 lb loaf tin with a long strip of nonstick paper; use some of the butter to grease the tin and paper well. Melt most of the remaining butter in a medium-sized saucepan, add the onion and fry for about 10 minutes until tender but not browned. Remove from the heat.

Grind the cashew nuts in a food processor with the bread and garlic, and add to the onion, together with the water or stock, salt, pepper, grated nutmeg and lemon juice to taste.

Mix all the stuffing ingredients together.

Put half the cashew nut mixture into the prepared tin, top with the stuffing, then spoon the rest of the nut mixture on top. Dot with the remaining butter. Stand the tin in another tin to catch any butter which may ooze out, and bake for about 30 minutes, or until firm and lightly browned. (Cover the roast with foil if it gets too brown before then.)

Cool for a minute or two in the tin, then slip a knife around the sides, turn the nut roast out and strip off the paper. Decorate with sprigs of parsley and small slices of lemon, and surround with roast potatoes, if you're serving them.

OPPOSITE: *Christmas Dinner 1, with Cashew Nut Roast with Herb Stuffing*

CHESTNUT AND RED WINE PÂTÉ EN CROÛTE

MENU 2

Iced Melon Soup with Violets

~

Chestnut and Red Wine Pâté en Croûte
Horseradish Sauce · Vegetarian Gravy
Light Mashed Potatoes
Julienne of Root Vegetables

~

Rum-Marinated Fruits with
Coconut and Lime Cream
or Chocolate and Vanilla Ice Cream

~

Mince Pies

~

WINES: *Chardonnay (white) Côtes du Rhône
or Cabernet Shiraz (red)*

ICED MELON SOUP WITH VIOLETS

2 ogen melons, or 1 large
 honeydew melon
2 tbls caster sugar

small bunch of fresh
 violets, washed and
 very gently shaken
 dry

Halve the melons and remove the seeds. Scoop out the flesh and liquidize until smooth, adding a little sugar if necessary. Chill in the fridge until ready to serve.

Serve the soup in chilled bowls, garnished with a few violet heads floating in each one. Or for extra effect, serve from one large bowl set over a larger bowl of crushed ice.

25 g/1 oz butter or vegan
 margarine
2 medium-sized onions,
 chopped
2 garlic cloves, crushed
50 g/2 oz button
 mushrooms, sliced
 (optional)
75 ml/3 fl oz red wine

$\frac{1}{2}$ × 375 g/12 oz can
 unsweetened chestnut
 purée or mashed fresh or
 canned chestnuts
75 g/3 oz soft fresh white
 or brown breadcrumbs
salt and freshly ground
 black pepper
450 g/1 lb Quick Flaky
 Pastry (page 29)
a little beaten egg to glaze
 (optional)

Melt the butter in a medium-large saucepan, add the onions and fry for about 10 minutes, until tender but not browned. Add the garlic and mushrooms, if you're using them, and cook for a further 2–3 minutes. Pour in the wine and let it bubble away for a minute or two until most of the liquid has gone; then remove from the heat and stir in the chestnut purée, breadcrumbs and salt and pepper to taste.

Set the oven to 230°C/450°F/Gas Mark 8.

On a lightly floured board, roll out the pastry into two strips, one measuring about 15 × 30 cm/6 × 12 inches; the other 22 × 30 cm/9 × 12 inches. Put the smaller strip on to a baking sheet brushed with cold water. Spoon the chestnut mixture on to the pastry, keeping 1 cm/$\frac{1}{2}$ inch clear all round the edges, and piling it up well into a nice loaf-like shape in the middle. Brush the edges of the pastry with cold water, then ease the second piece of pastry on top; press down lightly and trim the edges. Cut the trimmings into holly leaves, Christmas trees, bells or whatever you fancy, and stick them on top of the pastry with water. Make a few small steam holes, then brush with beaten egg if you're using this.

Put into the oven and bake for 7–8 minutes, then reduce the temperature to 200°C/400°F/Gas Mark 6 and bake for a further 20–25 minutes.

OPPOSITE: *Christmas Dinner 2, with Chestnut and Red
Wine Pâté en Croûte*

CHERRY TOMATOES WITH HORSERADISH CREAM

450 g/1 lb cherry
tomatoes
salt and freshly ground
pepper
dash of sugar

4 tbls plain yogurt
1 tbls mayonnaise
1–3 tsp creamed
horseradish
fresh basil leaves

Cover the cherry tomatoes with boiling water; leave for a few seconds until the skins have loosened, then drain and cover the tomatoes with cold water. Slip off the skins with a small sharp knife. Put the tomatoes into a bowl and season with a little salt, pepper and a dash of sugar, if they need it. Chill until required.

Mix together the yogurt, mayonnaise and horseradish; season lightly and chill this, too.

Just before you want to serve this dish, put the tomatoes on to six individual serving dishes. Spoon the yogurt mixture over them and garnish with whole or shredded basil leaves.

STUFFED ACORN SQUASH

For this Christmas Dinner with an American flavour, you can either use small acorn squash, allowing half for each person, or one bigger one, depending on what is available. I think small ones are particularly good, but the combination of firm, buttery squash and light nutty filling is delicious either way.

2 small squash – about
350–450 g/12–16 oz
each, or 1 larger one,
700–900 g/1½–2 lb
25 g/1 oz butter or vegan
margarine
1 onion, chopped

1 small green chilli
(optional)
100 g/4 oz whole cashew
nuts, lightly chopped
2 tbls desiccated coconut
1 tbls chopped parsley
salt and freshly ground
black pepper

Halve the squash, scoop out the seeds and trim the bases a little as necessary so that they stand level. Cook them in water to cover for about 15 minutes – perhaps longer if you are using the bigger squash – or until you can pierce the flesh easily with a knife. Drain well and blot with kitchen paper. Stand the squash in an ovenproof dish or on a baking sheet and season with a little salt and pepper.

Next make the filling. Melt half the butter or margarine in a saucepan, add the onion and fry for 10 minutes, letting it brown a bit. Meanwhile, halve the chilli, if you're using this, and rinse away the seeds under the tap. Chop the chilli and add to the onion, along with the cashew nuts and coconut, and fry for a further 2–3 minutes. Season and pile the mixture into the squash. Cut the remaining butter into four pieces and put on top of the stuffing. Set the oven to 200°C/400°F/Gas Mark 6.

Cover the whole dish or tin with a piece of foil and bake the squash for about 15 minutes for small squash, 25–30 minutes for larger ones, or until heated through. Remove the foil and bake for a further 5–10 minutes, then serve immediately.

OPPOSITE: *Christmas Dinner 3, with Stuffed Acorn Squash*

MENU 4

Celery and Stilton Soup

~

Yuletide Ring with Parsley Stuffing Balls
Wild Mushroom and Madeira Sauce
Leeks Cooked in Spiced Wine
Cock's Comb Roast Potatoes · Carrot Purée

~

Exotic Fruit Salad and Lychee Sorbet

~

Mince Pies

~

WINES: *Fumé Blanc (white)*
Rioja or Shiraz (red)

CELERY AND STILTON SOUP

If you're going to freeze this soup, don't add the cheese. This can be grated, ready for adding, and frozen separately, to save time.

1 celery, or outside stalks
from 2 heads of celery —
about 450 g/1 lb in all
1 tbls olive oil
1 onion, chopped

1.5 l/2½ pints water or
stock
150–175 g/5–6 oz
Stilton cheese, grated
salt and freshly ground
black pepper

Remove and reserve any leaves from the celery stalks; then chop the celery. Heat the oil in a large saucepan, add the onion and celery and fry gently, with the lid on the pan, for about 10 minutes, until tender but not browned. Add the water or stock, bring to the boil, and let the soup simmer for about 30 minutes, or until the celery is completely cooked and soft.

Liquidize the soup to remove any stringy bits, and pour it through a sieve back into the pan. Heat the soup to boiling point, then remove from the heat and add the cheese and reserved celery leaves. Stir gently until the cheese has melted into the soup.

Quickly check the seasoning (you probably won't need much as Stilton cheese is quite salty) and serve into warmed bowls.

YULETIDE RING

This makes a dramatic centrepiece to a Christmas Dinner — and there's enough here to feed 12 people, or one serving hot and one cold, for six. It consists of an outer layer of savoury brown nut roast followed by a lemony white layer, and a moist mushroom pâté. I like to fill the middle of the ring with herby stuffing balls, which are always popular.

FOR THE OUTER LAYER
50 g/2 oz butter or vegan
margarine
1 large onion, chopped
90 g/3½ oz button
mushrooms
1 tsp mixed herbs
2 tomatoes, fresh or
canned
150 g/5 oz soft
wholewheat breadcrumbs
150 g/5 oz cashew nuts,
grated
150 g/5 oz walnuts,
grated
1 tbls Marmite
2 tbls soy sauce
salt and freshly ground
black pepper

FOR THE ALMOND AND
LEMON LAYER
50 g/2 oz butter or vegan
margarine
1 large onion, chopped
225 g/8 oz blanched
almonds
100 g/4 oz soft white
breadcrumbs
2 lemons

FOR THE MUSHROOM
PÂTÉ
450 g/1 lb button
mushrooms
25 g/1 oz butter
75 g/3 oz soft
breadcrumbs
butter for greasing tin
slices of lemon and
tomato, and sprigs of
parsley, to garnish

OPPOSITE: *Christmas Dinner 4, with Yuletide Ring with Parsley Stuffing Balls*

with butter, and scatter with nuts. Repeat with another layer, then a final layer of filo pastry, which you just brush with butter. Now tip the tomato filling mixture on top and spread it to about 2.5 cm/1 inch of the edges. Fold the edges over, to enclose the edge of the filling then, starting from one of the widest edges, roll the whole thing up like a Swiss Roll, trying not to let it break (although it's not the end of the world if it does). Brush with more melted butter, and garnish with some shreds or shapes of filo pastry.

Put the strudel into the oven and bake for 30 minutes, or until golden brown. Transfer carefully to a serving dish with the aid of two fish slices.

Cut the thick stalks from the broccoli, then peel off the outer skin and cut the stalks into matchsticks. Separate the florets, halving any larger ones, so that they are all roughly the same size.

When you are ready to cook the broccoli – just a few minutes before you want to eat it – bring 2.5 cm/1 inch of water to boil in a large saucepan. Add the broccoli, put a lid on the pan, and cook for 3 minutes; test it: it should be just tender when pierced with a knife. Immediately remove from the heat, drain – the water makes good stock – and put the broccoli back into the saucepan with the butter and some salt and freshly ground black pepper to taste.

CELERIAC AND POTATO PURÉE

225 g/8 oz celeriac
450 g/1 lb potatoes
25 g/1 oz butter or vegan margarine

3–4 tbls cream or soya milk
salt and freshly ground black pepper
parsley sprigs, to garnish

Peel the celeriac and potatoes and cut them into even-sized chunks. Put them into a saucepan, cover with water and boil until they are both tender, about 15 minutes. Drain them, keeping the liquid, then mash them thoroughly using a potato masher or by pushing them through a *mouli-legumes*. Add the butter or vegan margarine, the cream or soya milk, and enough of the cooking water to make a soft, creamy purée. Snip some parsley over the top.

BUTTERED BROCCOLI

450 g/1 lb broccoli
25 g/1 oz butter

salt and freshly ground black pepper

WHOLE BABY CARROTS

450 g/1 lb baby carrots, scrubbed
25 g/1 oz butter

squeeze of lemon juice
salt and freshly ground black pepper

These carrots are delicious cooked in a steamer, over another vegetable, such as potatoes. Watch them carefully as they cook quickly if they are really tiny – the timing will depend on the size, but could be as little as 4–5 minutes for really baby ones, while bigger carrots could take up to 15 minutes.

Drain the carrots, then return to the hot saucepan or put into a warmed serving dish. Add the butter, seasoning and a squeeze of lemon juice, and mix gently to distribute the butter.

FOR THE REMAINDER OF THE MENU

OPPOSITE: *Christmas Dinner 5, with Christmas Savoury Strudel*

polythene or a plate, leave to get completely cold, then peel off the charred skin. Liquidize the pepper, adding a little water if necessary, to make a smooth purée the consistency of double cream. Season with salt and pepper.

To make the green sauce, put the basil, pine nuts and garlic into a blender and whizz to a purée, then add the oil and lastly the water.

Now for the rice. Wash the brown rice and the wild rice by putting them together in a sieve and rinsing under the cold tap. Put them into a saucepan with 450 ml/15 fl oz water and a good pinch of salt, and bring to the boil. Then cover the pan, turn the heat down very low and leave the rice to cook for 40 minutes, when it should be tender and all the water absorbed. If there's still some water, put the lid back on the pan and leave it to stand, off the heat, for another 15 minutes.

Meanwhile, wash the Basmati rice in the same way. This is best cooked in a panful of water, so put about 1.2 l/2 pints of water into a medium-large saucepan and bring to the boil, then add the rice and a good pinch of salt. Let the rice boil, uncovered, for about 10 minutes, or until it is just tender. Drain into a sieve and rinse with hot water. Add this rice to the brown rice mixture, together with the spring onions and salt and pepper as necessary. Mix it all gently with a fork, to avoid mashing the rice. Keep the rice warm over the lowest possible heat, perhaps using a heat-saving pad under the pan, or by standing the pan in an outer pan of boiling water.

To serve the rice, have ready a 1.2 litre/2 pint mould or six 200 ml/6–7 fl oz moulds – darioles, or little ramekins – lightly brushed with olive oil. Spoon in the rice and press down gently, then immediately turn it out on to a warmed serving plate or individual plates. Spoon the sauces in separate pools beside the rice, and garnish with a spring onion tassel or sprig of fresh tarragon.

FAVOURITE STIR-FRIED VEGETABLES

4 globe artichokes	3 tbls olive oil
lemon juice	salt and freshly ground
450 g/1 lb asparagus	black pepper
200–225 g/7–8 oz	squeeze of lemon juice
shitake mushrooms	90 g/3½ oz pine nuts,
225–250 g/8–9 oz oyster	lightly roasted under the
mushrooms	grill

First prepare the artichokes and asparagus, which can be done well in advance. Cut the leaves, stem and hairy choke from the artichokes, leaving just the bases. Squeeze a little lemon juice over the bases to preserve the colour, then put them into a saucepan, cover with water and simmer until just tender, about 15 minutes. Drain, cool, and cut into eighths.

While the artichokes are cooking, cut the tough stems off the asparagus, cut off the tips, and slice the stems slantwise into 2.5 cm/1 inch lengths. Bring 5 cm/2 inches of water to the boil in a saucepan and put in the asparagus. Boil it for about 2 minutes, or until it is bright green and still quite crisp. Drain both into a sieve and run the asparagus under cold water. Put the asparagus and the artichoke pieces into a bowl and cover with clingfilm until you need them.

To complete the stir-fry, wash and slice the shitake mushrooms; just wash the oyster mushrooms and pat dry on kitchen paper. Heat the oil in a large saucepan or wok if you have one, then put in the mushrooms. Cook for about 10 minutes, or until the mushrooms have softened, and any liquid has boiled away. Add the asparagus and artichokes and stir-fry gently for about 5 minutes, or until they are heated through. Add a squeeze of lemon juice and salt and pepper to taste, then serve, sprinkled with the pine nuts.

OPPOSITE: *Christmas Dinner 6, with Moulded Rice with Two Sauces*

CHRISTMAS SALAD

It is important that the cherry tomatoes are really firm, so that you can remove the skins without the tomatoes collapsing. If you can't get them, use 225 g/8 oz firm normal-size tomatoes instead, with the skin and the pulp removed, and the flesh cut into large dice. It's best to assemble this salad just before you want to serve it.

1 large creamy ripe avocado	*a few fresh basil leaves, roughly torn*
lemon juice	*1 tbls olive oil*
1 × 400 g/14 oz can palm hearts	*salt and freshly ground black pepper*
225 g/8 oz cherry tomatoes, skinned	

Peel, stone and slice the avocado; put the slices into a bowl and sprinkle with a little freshly squeezed lemon juice. Drain the palm hearts, cut them into 2.5 cm/1 inch slices, and add to the avocado, together with the tomatoes, basil, oil and some salt and pepper to taste.

Mix gently and serve immediately.

CREAMY POTATO SALAD

This salad is surprisingly light and delicate given its ingredients. Use either home-made mayonnaise or a good-quality bought one, such as Hellman's; if you can't find chives, use the green parts of spring onions very finely chopped.

700 g/1½ lb baby new potatoes	*1 tsp red wine or tarragon vinegar*
2 tbls mayonnaise	*1 tsp Dijon mustard*
2 tbls soured cream or thick yogurt	*salt and freshly ground black pepper*
	2 tbls finely chopped chives

Scrub the potatoes, and halve or quarter them unless they are very small. Put them into a saucepan, cover with water, bring to the boil, and boil for 7–10 minutes, or a bit more, depending on the size of the potatoes. They should be tender but not breaking up. Drain and set aside to cool (the water makes a very good stock).

To make the dressing, mix together the mayonnaise, soured cream or yogurt, vinegar and mustard, then pour this over the potatoes; stir gently so that they are all coated. Put the mixture into a shallow dish and sprinkle with the chives.

The potato mixture can be covered and kept in the fridge for 12–24 hours, but add the chives just before serving.

FOR THE REMAINDER OF THE MENU

Christmas Bombe   *page 120*
Mince Pies   *page 15*

MENU 6 COUNTDOWN

MAKE IN ADVANCE
Cream of Carrot Soup: freeze for 2–4 weeks.
Sesame Stars: freeze for 2–4 weeks.
Red Pepper Sauce: freeze for 2–4 weeks.
Christmas Bombe: make up to 14 days ahead, cover well and freeze.
Mince Pies: cook a batch and freeze (it's easiest to have a batch for heating on Christmas Day).

CHRISTMAS EVE
Remove from the freezer: Cream of Carrot Soup, Sesame Stars, Red Pepper Sauce. Put the Mince Pies on to a serving dish. Leave to thaw overnight.

Prepare the vegetables for the stir-fry; put them into separate polythene bags in the fridge. Toast the pine nuts. Make the rice mixture; keep in a glass or metal bowl (making it easier to reheat), cover. Cook the potatoes for the salad then cool before combining with the rest of the ingredients.

Make the Green Sauce; put into a serving dish, cover and keep in the fridge.

Get together serving dishes – a large one to hold the rice, either in little timbales or turned out of a large mould; jugs/bowls for the sauces; a round plate for the Christmas Bombe. Gather individual plates for the first course, main course and pudding.

CHRISTMAS DAY
11.00 am Lay the table. (This can be done on Christmas Eve if you're in the mood and don't need the table for breakfast.) Chill the white wine.

11.45 am Set the bowl of rice, covered with foil, over a pan of simmering water, to reheat. Prepare the garnish for the Moulded Rice.

12.15 pm Make the Christmas Salad; cover and keep in a cool place.

12.30 pm Open the red wine. Reheat the sauces, then serve them out and keep them warm in their pans over a very low heat. (Or stand the pans in a baking tin of steaming water over a low heat.) Turn the rice into small oiled dariole moulds, or one large mould. Keep warm in hot water over a hot plate or in a cool oven set to 150°C/300°F/Gas Mark 1.

12.45 pm Make the stir-fried vegetables. When they are done, turn off the heat. Put the Christmas Bombe into the fridge to soften it a bit.

12.55 pm Reheat the soup; put the sesame stars into a serving dish; open the white wine; light the candles.

1.00 pm Dinner is served!

After the starter Quickly serve out the sauces if you haven't already done so. Turn the heat on under the stir-fry and give the mixture another quick stir as it reheats (it should still be quite hot), then serve out and sprinkle with the pine nuts. Turn the rice out on to a warmed serving dish. Put the Mince Pies, covered in foil, towards the bottom of the oven to warm through. Take main course dishes to the table.

After the main course Sprinkle the Mince Pies with caster sugar and take to the table. Turn out the bombe and take it to the table.

FESTIVE PUDDINGS

Even if you eat abstemiously most of the year – perhaps, especially if – I think it's good to have something a bit different once a year, at Christmas. At the same time, many Christmas main courses are quite rich and filling, and for these, a light, yet still festive, pudding is required. So the recipes in this chapter range from the simple and refreshing, such as Lychee Sorbet, Christmas Dried Fruit Salad, Orange Slices with Flower Water, Exotic Fruit Salad and Figs with Raspberry Coulis, which are great to round off a substantial meal, to the luxurious and indulgent, such as Chocolate Charlotte with Chocolate Holly Leaves, Christmas Bombe and Meringue Nests with Several Fillings – all wonderful and wicked for those special occasions!

The dishes here can be mixed and matched with recipes in the rest of the book to make up menus suitable for various occasions over Christmas. For a balanced menu, it's best (though not essential, of course) to avoid serving a fruity pudding if you're having a fruit-based first course; and to avoid having a creamy pudding if the starter and/or main

course contain cream, or are particularly rich. And it's probably not a wonderful idea to serve a particularly filling nut roast with a scrumptiously hearty dish like Lemon Suprise Pudding. If you're uncertain which to aim for, you could solve the dilemma by providing a choice so that your guests can decide for themselves.

Some of these puddings make excellent alternatives to the traditional Christmas Pudding on Christmas Day (I've even included a special Light Christmas Pudding so that you can be both traditional *and* modern/healthy!); and a choice of two or more contrasting dishes will provide a great finale to a buffet or fork party. I'm not usually a pudding person, but sometimes for a special occasion over Christmas, I quite like having a portion of favourite pudding instead of a main meal, perhaps with some good strong black coffee – a real treat.

Your choice of 'big day' and party/buffet puddings is up to you, but you will make life easier for yourself if you choose something that doesn't require last-minute preparation. As with the savoury recipes in this book, most of the puddings here either freeze well or are easy to whizz up very quickly from fresh and/or storecupboard ingredients. The accent throughout is on minimal preparation – and maximum enjoyment!

LIGHT CHRISTMAS PUDDING

This pudding freezes well either cooked or uncooked – if you freeze cooked, defrost then cook for 45 minutes for large 35 minutes for small.

I've adapted this deliciously light, fruity pudding without any flour from Doris Grant's Christmas Pudding recipe in Food Combining For Health. *Unlike a traditional Christmas pudding, you make it just before you want to eat it (although you need to soak the prunes two days before), and steam for about three hours. Serve with Rum Sauce (page 29).*

90 g/3½ oz prunes
300 g/11 oz sultanas
200 g/7 oz large raisins, such as Lexia
75 g/3 oz finely chopped walnuts
juice of 1 small orange, and grated rind if untreated

100 g/4 oz ground almonds
90 ml/3 fl oz brandy
2 egg yolks
1 tsp mixed spice (optional)

Cover the prunes with plenty of water and leave them to soak for 2 days.

Drain them, saving the water, remove their stones and put the prunes into a food processor with half the sultanas and all but 50 g/2 ounces of the raisins. Whizz to a purée. Tip the mixture into a bowl and add the remaining raisins, the chopped walnuts, juice of the orange and rind if you're using this, the ground almonds, brandy, egg yolks and 150 ml/5 fl oz of the reserved prune water. For a spicy, traditional Christmas pudding flavour, add the mixed spice; without it, the pudding tastes rich and fruity. Mix well to a medium-soft consistency.

Grease the pudding basin(s) with butter, then spoon in the pudding mixture, leaving plenty of room at the top for it to rise. Cover with a circle of greaseproof paper, put on a lid if the basin has one or secure with some foil, or a pudding cloth over the top. Stand the pudding or puddings in a saucepan with boiling water to come two thirds of the way up the sides, and steam for 3 hours for the large pudding and 1½ hours for the small ones.

Loosen the edges and turn out on to a warmed serving dish or individual plates.

MAKES ONE 1.2 L/2 PINT PUDDING OR SIX 175 G/6 OZ ONES

GOOSEBERRY TARTLETS

These tartlets, a memory of sunny days past and a reminder of those to come, are good for post-Christmas eating, being a complete contrast to mince pies and other Christmas flavours. Serve with Apricot Coulis (page 26) to make it a real pudding.

1 quantity (250 g/9 oz) Rich Shortcrust Pastry, (page 29)
1 × 680 g/1½ lb jar gooseberries (about 375 g/12 oz drained weight)

caster sugar
1 tsp arrowroot or cornflour

Set the oven to 190°C/375°F/Gas Mark 5 and lightly grease six to eight 6–7 cm/2½–3 inch loose-base fluted flan tins with butter. On a lightly floured board, roll out the pastry thinly, and line the tins. Prick the bases lightly, then bake for 10–15 minutes, or until the pastry is set and golden brown. Remove from the oven and cool.

To make the gooseberry filling, drain the gooseberries well, keeping the liquid. Sweeten them if necessary with a little sugar – they should still have a nice sharp tang to them. Just before you want to serve the tartlets (but not too soon, or the gooseberries may make the pastry soggy), fill each pastry base with gooseberries.

Blend the arrowroot or cornflour with 150 ml/5 fl oz of the reserved gooseberry liquid, again sweetening to taste. Bring this to the boil in a small saucepan, stir for a minute or two until it has thickened, then take it off the heat and pour a little over the fruit in each tartlet. It will set almost immediately, and they are then ready. To serve them as a pudding, serve warm on individual plates, with a pool of apricot coulis beside them.

MAKE 6–8 TARTLETS

OPPOSITE: *Light Christmas Pudding with Rum Sauce, page 29*

FLOATING ISLANDS

I love this light and delicately flavoured pudding, which I find perfect for serving during the Christmas season, a welcome contrast to Christmas Pudding. It's excellent served just as it is or can be topped with some cinnamon-flavoured caramel (as here).

2 egg whites	300 ml/10 fl oz single
100 g/4 oz caster sugar,	cream
preferably from a jar	300 ml/10 fl oz milk
with a vanilla pod in it	1 vanilla pod
	4 egg yolks
	2 tsp cornflour

Whisk the egg whites until they stand in stiff peaks, then whisk in all but 1 tablespoonful of the sugar. Put the cream and milk into a large saucepan with the vanilla pod and bring to simmering point. Drop walnut-sized pieces of the meringue mixture into the milk and cream, allowing room for them to double in size. Simmer gently for about 3 minutes, until the meringues are set and firm. Carefully lift them out with a perforated spoon, and place on kitchen paper. Continue until all the egg white is used – you will probably end up with about 18 meringues.

Now put the 4 egg yolks into a small bowl with the cornflour and the remaining sugar. Add a little of the milk and cream from the pan, mixing until smooth, then tip this in with the rest of the milk and cream. Stir over a gentle heat until the mixture will coat the back of a wooden spoon – don't let it boil – then remove from the heat and pour into a shallow glass serving dish. Put the meringues on top.

Leave until cool, then chill for at least 30 minutes before serving – several hours is better.

If you want to add a caramel topping, heat 50 g/2 oz granulated sugar in a small pan until melted and golden brown, then remove from the heat, stir in $\frac{1}{2}$ teaspoon powdered cinnamon, and pour over the meringues before chilling.

SERVES 6

OPPOSITE: *(right) Floating Islands and (left) Christmas Dried Fruit Salad, page 112*

SNOWY TRIFLE

I don't make trifle very often, but when I do, I like to make it with a home-made Swiss roll and proper, vanilla-flavoured, egg custard. The result is a light, delicate, very 'snowy' and absolutely delectable dessert.

1 large raspberry Swiss	4 egg yolks or 1 egg and
roll (page 132)	2 yolks
4 tbls sherry or sweet	40 g/1½ oz caster sugar
wine	2 tsp cornflour
	300 ml/10 fl oz whipping
FOR THE CUSTARD	cream
600 ml/1 pint milk	50 g/2 oz flaked almonds,
1 vanilla pod	toasted

First, make the custard. Put the milk into a saucepan with the vanilla pod and bring to the boil. Remove from the heat, cover and leave to infuse for about 15 minutes.

Meanwhile, whisk together the eggs, sugar and cornflour, just to blend. Strain the milk on to the egg mixture, then pour the whole lot back into the saucepan and stir over a gentle heat for a few minutes until the mixture thickens – don't let it boil. It's done when it's thick enough to coat the spoon thinly. When you get to that point, take it off the heat and leave on one side for the moment. (Wash and dry the vanilla pod – it can be used many times.)

Cut the Swiss roll into slices, put these into a wide shallow dish, preferably glass, and sprinkle the sherry on top. Strain the custard over the top, then put it into the fridge to chill for about an hour, and to allow it to set a bit. Once this has happened, whip the cream and spread it lightly all over the top.

Chill until required; sprinkle the toasted almonds on top just before serving.

SERVES 6

CHOCOLATE CHARLOTTE WITH CHOCOLATE HOLLY LEAVES

This amount is right for a 20 cm/8 inch loose-base tin, serving 14 people – a real party piece. For a smaller charlotte, to serve 6, use an 18 cm/7 inch tin, and halve all the ingredients except for the sponge fingers; you'll still need more than one packet. The holly leaves are quite difficult to make. Use very flat leaves if you can find them, and get the chocolate really thick. They need to be as cold as possible to peel off, but can't be put in the fridge. If you find them really impossible, an alternative is to cut holly leaf shapes from a thin sheet of melted chocolate – but those lack the pretty curves and veins of the actual leaves. I found Meunier cooking chocolate worked particularly well.

FOR THE HOLLY LEAVES
100 g/4 oz plain
  chocolate
10 or more holly leaves,
  not too hard or curvy

FOR THE CHARLOTTE
2 × 200 g/7 oz packets of
  sponge finger biscuits

6 tbls rum
450 g/1 lb plain
  chocolate, broken up
600 ml/1 pint single
  cream
150 ml/5 fl oz whipping
  cream, whipped with 1
  tablespoon rum, to
  decorate

The holly leaves can be made some time in advance if you wish; they will keep in a tin, with greaseproof paper between the layers. The leaves should be clean and completely dry. Melt the chocolate then, holding a leaf by its stem, pull it through the chocolate, until the top is covered. Make sure it is really thick. Leave it, chocolate side up, until completely cold and set – overnight is best. (Don't put the leaves into the fridge, or you might get white spots on them.) Once they are completely set, peel the leaves away from the chocolate.

To make the charlotte itself, first prepare the tin. If you haven't got a loose-base tin, line an ordinary one by pressing foil into it to cover the base and sides. Arrange sponge finger biscuits all round the edge of the tin, then sprinkle half the rum in the base and arrange more sponge fingers over the base, to cover it, more or less, breaking them as necessary to fit. They don't have to be neat. Sprinkle the rest of the rum evenly on top.

Next, make the filling. Put the chocolate and single cream into a bowl set over a saucepan of simmering water and heat gently until the chocolate has melted. Remove from the heat and cool quickly by placing the bowl in a bowl of cold water. Once it is cold and beginning to set, whisk it hard until it's thick and light – an electric whisk is best for this. (If it refuses to go thick, it isn't cold enough. Put the bowl back in cold water for a few minutes longer.)

Carefully spoon the chocolate mixture into the tin, pushing the sponge finger biscuits back against the sides of the tin if they flop forwards. Chill in the fridge until firm.

To serve, remove the charlotte from the tin. If you've used the tin lined with foil, carefully lift the foil out, then peel down the sides. Slide a fish slice under the charlotte and lift it on to a serving dish.

Decorate with whipped cream and holly leaves and a dusting of grated chocolate; add a ribbon around the outside of the Charlotte, too, if you want an extra festive touch.

SERVES 14

OPPOSITE: *Chocolate Charlotte with Chocolate Holly Leaves*

ORANGE SLICES WITH FLOWER WATER

This deliciously refreshing salad is best made ahead of serving, to allow the flavours to mellow — it can be made a day or two in advance and kept in the fridge, well covered. Remove from the fridge for an hour or so before serving. Serve with Vegan Cream (page 26) for a luxurious yet light pudding.

9 oranges   orange flower water
honey — Greek, or orange
flower if possible

Scrub one of the oranges thoroughly then, preferably with a zester, pare off long thin strips of peel. Keep on one side.

Holding the oranges over a bowl, use a sharp, serrated stainless steel knife to cut away the peel and zest together, round and round, like peeling an apple in one go. Slice the orange flesh into thin circles or segments. Add the zest. Sweeten to taste with a little honey and add the orange flower water.

Cover and leave until ready to serve.
SERVES 6

CHRISTMAS DRIED FRUIT SALAD

Add a tablespoon of orange flower water to this dried fruit salad to give it extra fragrance.

This is very easy to make and good to eat — it's lovely with the Floating Islands (page 109) or with thick Greek yogurt. You can either buy packets of mixed dried fruit, or make your own combination, including raisins, figs, or whatever you fancy.

450 g/1 lb mixed dried   1 cinnamon stick, broken
fruit — peaches, apricots,   in half
prunes, pears, apples   6 tbls rum or brandy
50 g/2 oz soft brown or   90 g/3½ oz blanched
demerara sugar   almonds

Wash the dried fruit, then put it into a bowl, cover with plenty of water and leave to soak overnight. Next day put into a saucepan with its soaking water

and more, if necessary, to make it just level with the top of the fruit. Add the sugar and cinnamon stick and bring to the boil. Let the mixture simmer away, without a lid on the pan, for about an hour, or until nearly all the liquid has boiled away.

Remove from the heat and add the rum and nuts. Leave to cool, then serve at room temperature.
SERVES 4–6

MERINGUE NESTS WITH SEVERAL FILLINGS

12 Meringue Nests (page   FRUIT FILLING
26)   fresh fruit, such as
          strawberries, kiwi,
ORANGE LIQUEUR AND   grapes, etc
GLACÉ FRUIT FILLING   150 ml/5 fl oz whipping
150 ml/5 fl oz whipping   cream
cream
1 tsp grated orange rind   GINGER FILLING
2 tbls orange liqueur   150 ml/5 fl oz whipping
red and yellow glacé   cream
fruits, to decorate   25 g/1 oz chopped stem
chopped angelica, to   ginger
decorate   chocolate curls and grated
          chocolate, to decorate

To make the orange liqueur and glacé fruit filling, beat the cream until thick, then stir in the orange rind and liqueur. Pile into four meringue nests and decorate with glacé fruits and angelica.

To make the fruit filling, chop your selection of fresh fruit and whip the cream until thick; divide between four nests.

To make the ginger filling, beat the cream until thick, then stir in two-thirds of the stem ginger. Spoon into the remaining nests and use the rest of the ginger and the chocolate to decorate the tops.
SERVES 3–6

OPPOSITE: *Meringue Nests with Several Fillings*

LYCHEE SORBET

This is a pudding which can be whizzed up in no time at all, and it is fragrant and refreshing.

2 × 410 g/14 oz cans lychees in syrup
juice and grated rind of 1 lemon
2 egg whites
fresh violets, jasmine, or mint leaves, to decorate

Drain the lychees, keeping the liquid. Put the lychees into a food processor with the lemon juice and rind and 300 ml/10 fl oz of the reserved liquid, and whizz to a purée. Pour this into a shallow container and freeze until the mixture is half-frozen, about 2 hours.

Whizz again in a liquidizer. Whisk the egg whites until stiff, then beat in the lychee purée. Pour the mixture back into the freezing container, and freeze for about 3 hours, until firm.

Remove the sorbet from the freezer about 45 minutes before you want to eat it, then put several scoops into individual glass dishes.
SERVES 6

VEGAN VERSION
Simply omit the egg whites and whisk extra vigorously!

FIGS WITH RASPBERRY COULIS

An out-of-season treat . . . If you can get fresh ripe figs at Christmas, and have some Raspberry Coulis (page 29) stashed away in the freezer, this pudding is light, easy and delicious.

You need one fresh fig for each person, 2–3 tablespoons of raspberry coulis and, if you like, a good heaped dessertspoonful of thick Greek yogurt. Wash the figs and pat them dry on kitchen paper. Cut

them downwards, through the stem but not completely through the base, making three cuts, so that you end up with six segments still attached to the base. Serve with a little pool of coulis and yogurt if you're using this.

EXOTIC FRUIT SALAD

This is one of the simplest, prettiest and most refreshing puddings, and makes a lovely contrast to some of the richer and more filling Christmas and winter dishes. Choose your own selection of fruits, aiming for plenty of different colours and textures. I think they look best arranged on a round glass plate, and they are delicious eaten on their own, or with thick Greek yogurt or, best of all, a scoopful of Lychee Sorbet (left).

6 lychees
1 ripe paw-paw or 2 pomegranates
1 nectarine
2 figs
50 g/2 oz Cape gooseberries
225 g/8 oz strawberries
100 g/4 oz raspberries, golden or red
1 star fruit
a few sprigs of fresh mint, to decorate

Using a stainless knife which won't give the fruit a metallic flavour, peel the lychees and paw-paw, and remove the stones. Remove the stone from the nectarine. Cut the flesh into neat pieces, not too small. If you are using pomegranates, halve them then, holding each half over a bowl to catch the delicious crimson juice, ease out the seeds with a small pointed teaspoon (a grapefruit spoon is ideal), or the point of a knife. Discard the skin. Slice the figs into thin circles. Pull back the petals on the Cape gooseberries, wash the strawberries and raspberries – and wash, then thinly slice, the star fruit. Arrange each type of fruit in a pile on a large platter, then decorate with a few sprigs of fresh mint.
SERVES 6

OPPOSITE: *(top) Lychee Sorbet and (below) Exotic Fruit Salad*

LEMON AND GINGER CHEESECAKE

I call this cheesecake, but really it's a bit of a cheat one, because it doesn't contain cheese — just a beautifully smooth, lemony cream (which sets like a cheesecake), on a crisp ginger-biscuit base. It's easy to make and an unfailingly popular party dessert. It's rich, so a little goes a long way.

200 g/7 oz ginger biscuits
75 g/3 oz butter
½ tsp ground ginger
300 ml/10 fl oz double
 cream

1 × 218 g/8 oz can
 condensed milk
grated rind and juice of 1
 lemon
slivers of lemon peel and
 chopped preserved ginger,
 to decorate

Crush the biscuits to coarse crumbs with a rolling pin. Melt the butter in a medium saucepan, then stir in the crushed biscuits and the ground ginger. Press this mixture into the base of an 18–20 cm/7–8 inch springform cake tin — the base of a clean jam jar is useful for pressing the crumbs firmly into the tin. Put into the fridge to chill.

Now make the filling: whisk the double cream until it is almost fully whipped, then add the condensed milk and whisk again, until very thick. Finally, stir in the lemon rind and juice. The mixture may look as if it's going to separate at first, but don't worry, it won't; just keep on stirring gently until it is very smooth and thick.

Spoon this mixture on top of the ginger base, then smooth and level it with the back of a spoon or a spatula. Cover and chill for several hours, then remove the outside of the springform tin and decorate the top of the cheesecake with lemon peel and ginger before serving.

This cheesecake can be made at least 24 hours in advance; it keeps very well for several days in the fridge, but keep it tightly covered so that it doesn't absorb any other flavours.
SERVES 8–12

RUM–MARINATED FRUITS WITH COCONUT AND LIME CREAM

1 ripe pineapple
2 bananas
1 ripe paw-paw
grated rind and juice of 1
 lime
50 g/2 oz brown sugar

4 tbls brown rum
100 g/4 oz coconut cream
300 ml/10 fl oz boiling
 water
extra sugar or honey to
 taste

Cut the skin from the pineapple, making sure you've taken out all the little black bits, remove the central core, and cut the flesh into dice. Skin and slice the bananas into chunks, peel and slice the paw-paw and add them to the pineapple, with half the lime juice, the sugar and rum. Cover and leave the mixture to marinate for at least 1 hour, stirring gently from time to time.

Meanwhile, make the cream. Cut up the coconut cream and put into a small saucepan with the boiling water. Stir until dissolved, heating gently if necessary. Then remove from the heat and leave until completely cold.

Stir in the lime rind and remaining juice, and a little sugar or honey to taste. It will thicken as it gets cold. Serve with the fruit.
SERVES 6

OPPOSITE: *Rum-Marinated Fruits with Coconut and Lime Cream*

CHRISTMAS BOMBE

When you cut this snowy white ice cream bombe, a golden inner layer flecked with brightly-coloured crystallized fruits is revealed. It's wonderful as an alternative Christmas pudding, or for a party, and it's easy to make. You need to allow plenty of time for the freezing — it's better to start making it the day before you need it, or it can be made up to four weeks in advance and stored in the freezer. It looks good with extra Cointreau-soaked crystallized fruits on top, but this makes the pudding quite boozy, so drivers should be warned!

FOR THE WHITE LAYER
4 egg whites
225 g/8 oz caster or
  vanilla sugar
150 ml/5 fl oz water
400 ml/15 fl oz whipping
  cream
a few drops of vanilla
  essence

FOR THE GOLDEN LAYER
225 g/8 oz crystallized
  fruits, in a variety of
  colours
2 tbls Cointreau or other
  orange liqueur
4 egg yolks
4 tangerines or satsumas
100 g/4 oz caster sugar
150 ml/5 fl oz whipping
  cream
extra glacé fruit, to
  decorate

First turn your freezer to its coldest setting and chill a 1.5 l/3 pint ice cream bombe mould or pudding basin, preferably metal.

Now for the white ice cream. Put the egg whites into a bowl and whisk them until they are very stiff, as if you were making meringues. Put the caster sugar into a saucepan with the water and heat gently until the sugar has dissolved, then bring to the boil and boil hard for 3 minutes. Take off the heat and immediately pour this mixture on to the egg whites, whisking them at the same time. An electric table or hand whisk makes this operation easier. Next, whisk the cream until it will stand in soft peaks, then whisk it into the egg white mixture, together with a few drops of vanilla essence. Pour the whole lot into the bombe mould or bowl and freeze until firm — this may take 5–6 hours. Meanwhile, prepare the crystallized fruits; cut them into 1 cm/½ inch chunks then put them into a shallow container and sprinkle with the Cointreau.

Now make the tangerine ice cream for the 'golden' layer. Put the egg yolks into a bowl with the grated rind of two of the tangerines and whisk until pale and beginning to thicken. Squeeze the juice from all the tangerines and put this into a saucepan with the caster sugar. Heat gently until the sugar has dissolved, then boil hard for 3 minutes. Immediately pour this mixture over the egg yolks, whisking at the same time. When it has all been added, continue to whisk the mixture for about 5 minutes until it is very thick and light. Whisk the cream to the soft peak stage, then whisk this into the tangerine mixture. Put it into the freezer and freeze for 2–3 hours, or until it is beginning to solidify but is still soft enough to stir. Add the crystallized fruits and orange liqueur to the tangerine ice cream, together with any liquid that's left over.

Hollow out the inside of the white ice cream to make a cavity for the tangerine ice. Push the bits of ice cream that you scoop out of the centre up the sides of the bombe, aiming for a thickness of about 1cm/½ inch, although this will depend on the exact shape of your mould or bowl. Spoon the tangerine mixture into the centre and finish by smoothing any remaining white ice cream on top. Put the bombe back in the freezer and freeze for several hours until the layers are completely firm.

Unmould the bombe by dipping the mould into a bowl of hot water for a few seconds, then loosening the edges with a palette knife and turning the ice cream out on to a plate. Smooth the top with a palette knife, then put the bombe back into the freezer until you need it. Decorate with a few pieces of glacé fruit on top. It can be served straight from the freezer as it soon softens.

SERVES 8

OPPOSITE: *Christmas Bombe*

BOOZY VEGAN ICE CREAM

This is a simple vegan chocolate ice cream, which has always been a favourite with my kids, dressed up for Christmas with the addition of some dried fruits, nuts and booze. It makes a good frozen Christmas pudding if you freeze it in a plastic pudding basin.

1 tbls cornflour	100 g/4 oz glacé cherries
900 ml/1½ pints soya milk	50 g/2 oz whole mixed
1 vanilla pod	peel
2 tbls sugar	50 g/2 oz raisins or
50 g/2 oz vegan	sultanas
margarine	4 tbls rum or brandy
100 g/4 oz plain	25 g/1 oz flaked almonds
chocolate	

Put the cornflour into a bowl and blend to a paste with a little of the milk. Put the rest of the milk into a saucepan with the vanilla pod, sugar, margarine and the chocolate, broken into pieces. Heat gently to boiling point, then pour over the cornflour and mix until combined.

Return the mixture to the saucepan and bring to the boil, stirring. Remove from the heat. Cover and leave until cool, then remove the vanilla pod (wash and dry it – it can be used many times) and liquidize the mixture. Pour it into a container and freeze until it is solid around the edges. Whisk and return to the freezer. Repeat this process, this time whisking in the fruits and rum or brandy, and let the ice cream freeze until solid.

Make sure this ice cream is well-softened before you use it, as it freezes very hard – an hour at room temperature is not too long. Then beat it before serving, or simply turn it out of a pudding bowl, like a Christmas pudding.

SERVES 6–8

CHOCOLATE ICE CREAM

2 egg whites	100 g/4 oz dark
150 g/5 oz caster sugar	chocolate, broken up
8 tbls water	300 ml/10 fl oz whipping
	cream

Whisk the egg whites until they are stiff, as if you were making meringues. Next, put the sugar and water into a small saucepan and heat gently until the sugar has dissolved. Raise the heat and let the mixture boil for 2 minutes. Remove from the heat, and pour this over the egg whites, whisking at the same time.

Melt the chocolate in a bowl set over a pan of simmering water, or in the microwave, and add carefully and gradually to the egg white mixture. Whip the cream until it is standing in soft peaks, then fold quickly into the mixture.

Turn the ice cream into a polythene container and freeze until firm.

To serve, remove from the freezer 10–15 minutes before you need it, to soften it a little, and scoop into sundae glasses.

Decorate with extra chocolate (white makes a nice contrast, shaved into curls on a potato peeler as here) and biscuits, such as Macaroons (page 148).
SERVES 6

OPPOSITE: *Chocolate Ice Cream and Macaroons, page 148*

LAST–MINUTE CHRISTMAS CAKE

If you can't find small cake tins, make the little cakes by cutting the big square one into quarters then carefully sculpting into rounds.

575 g/1¼ lb mixed dried
fruit
225 g/8 oz sultanas
225 g/8 oz Lexia raisins
grated rind and juice of 1
lemon
1 tbls black treacle
150 ml/5 fl oz port or
sherry

250 g/9 oz wholewheat
flour and plain white
flour, mixed
1 tsp mixed spice
1 tsp powdered cinnamon
225 g/8 oz butter
225 g/8 oz dark brown
sugar
4 eggs
175 g/6 oz glacé cherries
25 g/1 oz flaked almonds

Put the mixed dried fruit, sultanas, raisins, rind and juice and treacle into a saucepan with the port and bring to the boil. Remove from the heat, cover and leave to get cold. (This process can be speeded up if you stand the pan in a bowl of cold water.)

Meanwhile, set the oven to 150°C/300°F/Gas Mark 2 and line a 20 cm/8 inch square tin or four 10 cm/4 inch round tins with greaseproof paper.

Sift the flours with the spices, on to a plate. Cream the butter and sugar until very light, then alternately beat in the fruit, eggs and flour. Finally, stir in the cherries and almonds. Spoon the mixture into the tin or tins, hollowing out the centre very slightly so that the surface will be flat. Bake the large cake for 2–3 hours and the small ones for 1½–1¾ hours, or until a skewer inserted in the middle comes out clean. (It took 2 hours 30 minutes to cook the large one, 1½ hours for the small ones in my oven.) Leave to cool in the tin(s).

MAKES ONE 20 CM/8 INCH SQUARE CAKE OR
FOUR INDIVIDUAL 10 CM/4 INCH ROUND CAKES

TO PUT A NUTTY TOPPING ON THE SQUARE CAKE

This is a very quick, easy and effective topping for a Christmas Cake, especially nice if you aren't too keen on almond paste and icing. The nuts should be put on the cake before it's baked.

Hollow out the centre of the cake slightly so that it will be flat when it's cooked, then arrange the nuts attractively in diagonal rows on top; be careful not to press them into the mixture or they may sink and disappear as it bakes! For a 20 cm/8 inch cake with a separate row of each one, you will need about 50 g/2 ounces of blanched almonds, brazilnuts, skinned hazelnuts, pecan nuts or walnuts. Glacé cherries would make an attractive centre row. Finish with a flourish by tying a bow of red ribbon around the sides.

TO DECORATE THE LITTLE ROUND CAKES

Cover the cakes with almond paste (page 10), then make one recipe of Fondant Icing and use it to decorate the cakes (page 12).

For the mini-cakes shown here, I decorated the top of one cake with marzipan fruits (page 153), another with a mixture of glacé cherries, strips of angelica and crystallized orange segments and a third with a candle and some holly. For the fourth cake, I rerolled the fondant icing trimmings and cut into star shapes, using a pastry cutter, then used them to decorate the sides and top, dusting the top one with a little fine brown sugar. The final flourish is achieved by pinning an appropriately festive ribbon round the sides.

OPPOSITE: *Little Christmas Cakes*

LIGHT GINGER CAKE WITH LEMON ICING

I think this light ginger cake, with its tangy lemon icing, is nicer at Christmas than the more usual dark gingerbread because it's so different from Christmas Cake. It's very quick to make.

100 g/4 oz 85% wholewheat self-raising flour
1 tsp baking powder
2 tsp ground ginger
100 g/4 oz caster sugar
100 g/4 oz soft butter
2 eggs

50–100 g/2–4 oz preserved stem ginger, roughly chopped

FOR THE LEMON ICING
100 g/4 oz icing sugar
1–2 tbls freshly squeezed lemon juice
zest of lemon, to decorate

Set the oven to 170°C/325°F/Gas Mark 3 and line a 450 g/1 lb loaf tin with a strip of nonstick paper to cover the base and narrow sides; grease the uncovered sides with butter.

Sift the flour, baking powder and ginger into a food processor, mixer or bowl, then put in the sugar, butter and eggs. Whizz, whisk, or beat everything together until it is light, thick and slightly glossy looking. This will take about 3 minutes by hand, less time in a processor or with an electric whisk or mixer. Stir in the chopped stem ginger.

Spoon the mixture into the tin and gently level the top with the back of a spoon. Bake for 1 hour to 1 hour 10 minutes, or until the cake is risen, has shrunk a little from the sides of the tin, and the centre springs back to a light touch. Cool for a few minutes in the tin, then turn out on to a wire rack to finish cooling.

To make the icing, sift the icing sugar into a bowl, then gradually mix in enough of the lemon juice to make a stiff mixture. Put this on top of the cake, spreading it gently to the edges. Use a zester to make long thin strips of lemon peel, or shave off pieces of peel and cut them into long strips with a knife. Scatter these over the top of the cake.
MAKES ONE 450 G/1 LB CAKE

OPPOSITE: *Light Ginger Cake with Lemon Icing*

PARKIN

This parkin is a favourite recipe which has appeared before, but I wanted to include it as it's a useful cake for Christmas, contrasting well with other flavours and storing well – it can be made at least a week in advance and just goes on improving. One reader tells me that she always makes this parkin for her Christmas cake! It can be jazzed up with some glacé icing, and I love it with bits of chopped candied peel and preserved ginger in it (the kind in a pretty jar) but my kids all prefer it plain.

100 g/4 oz plain 100% wholemeal flour
2 tsp baking powder
2 tsp ground ginger
100 g/4 oz medium oatmeal
3 rounded tbls real barbados sugar
100 g/4 oz black treacle
100 g/4 oz golden syrup or honey

100 g/4 oz butter or vegan margarine
175 ml/6 fl oz milk or soya milk

OPTIONAL EXTRAS
50 g/2 oz preserved ginger, chopped
50 g/2 oz whole candied peel, chopped

Set the oven to 180°C/350°F/Gas Mark 4 and line a 20 cm/8 inch square tin with greased greaseproof paper.

Sift the flour, baking powder and ginger into a bowl, adding the residue of bran from the sieve, as well, and also the oatmeal. Put the sugar, treacle, golden syrup and butter or vegan margarine into a saucepan and heat gently until melted. Let the mixture cool until tepid, then add the milk to it. Pour the whole lot into the dry ingredients, and add the preserved ginger and candied peel if you're using these. Mix well, then pour into the prepared tin.

Bake for 50–60 minutes, or until the parkin is firm to the touch. Lift the parkin out of the tin, on its paper, and put it on a wire rack to cool. When it's cool, cut the parkin into pieces and remove the paper.
MAKES 12–16 PIECES

FAVOURITE SWISS ROLL

This log is particularly easy to make if you have a sugar thermometer.

This is a very light Swiss roll and it's very quick and easy to make if you have an electric whisk.

100 g/4 oz caster sugar	*1 tbls cornflour*
4 eggs	*225 g/8 oz raspberry jam*
50 g/2 oz self-raising	*extra cornflour and icing*
flour	*sugar, to dust*

The classic way to make a whisked sponge like this is to whisk the eggs and sugar over a pan of steaming water. However if you heat the sugar for a few minutes in the oven and then add this to the eggs, you can do away with the pan of water. So, first set the oven to 200°C/400°F/Gas Mark 6 and line a 22 × 32 cm/9 × 13 inch Swiss roll tin with greased greaseproof or nonstick paper. (Even nonstick paper needs to be greased for this recipe.)

Put the sugar on to a baking sheet and pop into the oven for 4–5 minutes to heat up. Break the eggs into a bowl or the bowl of an electric mixer, then tip in the sugar. Whisk for about 5 minutes, or until the mixture is very pale, light and fluffy, and the mixture will hold the impression of the whisk for several seconds. Then sift the flour and cornflour in on top, and fold them in carefully with a metal spoon or thin plastic spatula.

Pour the mixture into the prepared tin and bake for 7–8 minutes – it's done when the centre springs back to a light touch. While it's cooking, lay a piece of greaseproof paper or nonstick paper out on the working surface and dust it with cornflour, then turn the Swiss roll straight out on to this. Trim the short edges with a sharp knife.

Warm the jam gently in a saucepan, then pour and spread this all over the Swiss roll and quickly roll it up from one of the long edges. Brush off any excess cornflour, and dust with a little icing sugar.
MAKES ONE SWISS ROLL

BUCHE DE NOEL (CHOCOLATE LOG)

4 eggs	*100 g/4 oz caster sugar*
175 g/6 oz caster sugar	*150 ml/5 fl oz water*
2 egg whites	*100 g/4 oz plain*
50 g/2 oz cocoa powder	*chocolate, melted*
	100 g/4 oz soft unsalted
FOR THE SPECIAL	*butter*
BUTTERCREAM	*icing sugar*
2 egg yolks	

Set the oven to 200°C/400°F/Gas Mark 6 and line a greased 23 × 32 cm/9 × 13 inch Swiss roll tin with a piece of greased greaseproof paper.

First make the buttercream. Boil the sugar and water for 5 minutes. Meanwhile, whisk the egg yolks then pour in the sugar mixture and whisk well; add the chocolate, then gradually whisk in the butter. Chill then whip before using.

To make the log, whisk the eggs and sugar together in a bowl set over a pan of simmering water until they are pale and fluffy. Remove from the heat. Whisk the egg whites until stiff, then fold these gently into the mixture, too.

Pour the mixture into the prepared tin, spreading it out to the edges. Bake for 15 minutes. Cool mixture in the tin for 10 minutes, then cover with a damp teacloth and leave for a further 10 minutes. Remove the cloth and turn the cake out on to a piece of greaseproof paper that has been dusted with icing sugar. Remove the greaseproof paper from the top of the cake and leave to cool completely.

When the log is cold, trim the edges and spread the top with the whipped buttercream, then carefully roll the cake up like a Swiss roll, using the paper to help: don't worry if it cracks! Sprinkle with more icing sugar. This log will keep well in the fridge for several hours, and can also be frozen successfully.
SERVES 6–8

OPPOSITE: *Buche de Noel (Chocolate Log)*

SWEDISH RING CAKE

This makes a pleasant change from the rich and spicy food of Christmas, while still looking festive. It is also, for some reason I've never quite been able to understand, extremely popular with all children. (They might prefer it without the cinnamon — mine certainly do.)

75 g/3 oz butter
¾ tsp sugar
¾ tsp salt
200 ml/7 fl oz milk and
  boiling water, mixed
375 g/12 oz strong white
  flour
1 sachet easy-blend yeast
a little oil

50 g/2 oz demerara sugar
1 tsp powdered cinnamon
  (optional)

FOR THE GLACÉ ICING
225 g/8 oz icing sugar
squeeze of lemon juice
red and green glacé
  cherries, to decorate

Melt the butter without browning it, and leave to cool. Add the sugar and salt to the milk and water mixture, and stir until they have dissolved. Put the flour into a large bowl and sprinkle in the easy-blend yeast. Make a well in the centre. When the melted butter is tepid, pour this into the well, along with most of the milk and water mixture, which should also be tepid: too hot and it will kill the yeast, too cold, and it will take ages to work! Mix the flour into the liquid, adding the rest as necessary, until you have a sticky dough.

Now, either turn the dough out on to a lightly floured surface and knead it for 10 minutes, or divide it into batches and process it in a food processor with a dough blade for 1 minute. In either case, it's ready when it's smooth and has lost its stickiness. It should still be fairly soft. Oil the base of your mixing basin, put the ball of dough into this, then turn it up the other way so that the oily side is on top, to prevent a skin forming.

Put the bowl in a large carrier bag, closing it to exclude draughts, then leave it in a warm place. I generally stand it on a folded towel on a radiator and sometimes wrap a thick towel around it, too. Leave it for 1–2 hours, or until it has literally doubled in bulk. Then turn it out on to a lightly floured surface and knead it very briefly. Now press the dough out into a large rectangle, about 40 cm/16 inches long and 20 cm/8 inches across. Sprinkle the surface with the demerara sugar and the cinnamon if you're using this, then roll it up from one of longer edges and press the ends together to make a circle.

Place the ring on a baking sheet then, with scissors, make slanting cuts in the outer edge. Put the baking sheet inside the plastic bag again — or two bags, if it's large — and leave in a warm place for a further ¾–2 hours, or until the ring is very fat and puffy. It's really important to let it rise enough, then you'll get a lovely light, springy cake like the one pictured here.

About 20 minutes before you think this stage is reached, set the oven to 190°C/375°F/Gas Mark 5. Bake the cake for 30–35 minutes, then remove from the oven and set aside to cool on a wire rack, with a cloth over it to soften the crust.

Make the icing by mixing the icing sugar with a squeeze of lemon juice and enough cold water to make a thick, just-spreadable consistency. Spread this over the top of the cake, and decorate with slices of red and green glacé cherries.

MAKES ONE 20 CM/8 INCH RING

OPPOSITE: *(left) Swedish Ring Cake and (right) Little Christmas Buns, page 128*

CHRISTMAS 'FLOWERS'

This a great favourite with my family, particularly the kids. The 'flowers' are crisp biscuits, moulded into shape over a small cup while they are still warm; and the goodies inside can be as plain or partified as you like.

FOR THE 'FLOWERS'
25 g/1 oz butter or vegan
 margarine
50 g/2 oz icing sugar
25 g/1 oz plain flour
2–3 tbls double cream
1 egg white
icing sugar for dusting

FOR THE FILLING
vanilla ice cream
sweets
whipped double cream
seedless grapes
raspberries, blueberries
nectarines, etc

Set the oven to 200°C/400°F/Gas Mark 6. Draw four 10 cm/4 inch circles on a sheet of nonstick paper to fit a baking sheet.

Melt the butter, then mix it in with the icing sugar, flour, cream and egg white, beating well to make a smooth batter. Put a teaspoonful of this mixture on one of the circles, and spread it out carefully to cover the circle thinly. Make three more in the same way, then bake them for about 5 minutes, or until they are lightly browned. Set the unused mixture aside (you will use it later).

Have ready four small cups or jars (the size of mustard jars). Lift the biscuits off the paper and on to the inverted cups or jars, pressing the top to flatten it – this will be the base of the 'flower' and needs to be level so that it will stand well. Curve the edges round the cup or jar to shape. Leave to cool, then remove the biscuits. While the first lot are cooling, make more in the same way. These will keep for a day or two in an airtight tin, or carefully packed in a rigid container in the freezer.

To complete the 'flowers', stand them on a serving plate, or on individual plates and fill with tiny scoops of vanilla ice cream – a melon-baller is good for making these – lightly whipped cream and some little sweets or pieces of fruit.
MAKES 8 'FLOWERS'

OPPOSITE: *Christmas 'Flowers'*

BRANDY SNAPS

Everyone loves brandy snaps, and they're surprisingly easy to make. They harden as they cool, so the trick is to lift them off the paper as soon as they're firm enough to handle, but before they get too brittle to roll – so keep testing them. If they do get too hard, just pop them back in the oven for a few seconds to soften them up again. You can fill them with cream or ice cream, or serve them plain, with a creamy fool, fruit compôte or sorbet.

50 g/2 oz golden syrup
50 g/2 oz sugar
50 g/2 oz butter or
 margarine

50 g/2 oz plain flour
1 tsp ground ginger
1 tsp lemon juice

Set the oven to 200°C/400°F/Gas Mark 6, then line a large baking sheet with nonstick paper.

Put the golden syrup into a saucepan (you can measure it straight into the pan, if you have the kind of scales you can adjust), with the sugar and butter or margarine, and melt over a gentle heat. Take the pan off the heat and stir in the flour, ground ginger and lemon juice.

Put heaped teaspoons of the mixture well apart on the baking sheet (you'll probably need to do at least two batches). Bake for 4–6 minutes, or until the brandy snaps are an even mid-golden brown, then remove from the oven and leave to cool on the paper for 2–3 minutes.

As soon as the brandy snaps are firm enough to pick up with a fish slice, lift them off the paper and mould each around the handle of a wooden spoon, or some other suitable cylinder shape. When the brandy snaps are cool and crisp, remove them and keep them in an airtight tin until you need them. To serve them, fill with cream which has been whipped with a little brandy, or with vanilla ice cream.
MAKES 12 SNAPS

MIXED VEGETABLES IN OIL

This is an adaptation of one of Nicola Cox's delicious recipes from her lovely book Country Cooking. *You will need some jars with plastic-lined or glass lids; wash and sterilize the jars as described for Kumquats in Brandy (page 144). Choose a selection of the vegetables listed below.*

50 g/2 oz sea salt for
each 450 g/1 lb prepared
vegetables
450 g/1 lb baby carrots,
halved or quartered
downwards if fat
1 cucumber, cut into
chunky matchsticks
450 g/1 lb French beans,
topped and tailed
1 cauliflower, broken into
small florets

1 red pepper, seeded and
sliced into thin lengths
1 green pepper, seeded
and sliced into thin
lengths
12 baby pickling onions,
peeled
1 fennel, trimmed and cut
into lengthwise strips
fresh parsley sprigs
600 ml/1 pint spiced
vinegar (see below)
oil or grapeseed oil

Make up a brine by dissolving 50 g/2 oz of sea salt in a pint of water for every pound of vegetables. Put the vegetables into a deep glass or china bowl and pour over the brine to cover them. Put a plate and weight on top to keep the vegetables under water. Leave them there for 12–24 hours, then drain them and rinse them well under cold water.

Arrange the vegetables attractively in the sterilized jars, adding some fresh parsley sprigs too, and packing them firmly to within an inch of the tops of the jars. Then whisk 1 part spiced vinegar with 1 part light (not best virgin) olive oil and 1 part grapeseed oil and pour into the jars, to cover the vegetables and come right up to the top. Put on the lids, and leave for at least several days, preferably longer.

Take out the vegetables as you need them, making sure that the remaining vegetables are always covered by an inch of oil. (Later, the oil can be used in salad dressings, etc.)

MAKES ABOUT 1 KG/2 LB 2 OZ PICKLE

*If you overcook
this Apricot
Chutney and it gets
too thick and syrupy
stir in some cider
vinegar to thin it.*

SPICED VINEGAR

To make spiced vinegar, put 600 ml/1 pint of white wine vinegar into a saucepan with a couple of peeled garlic cloves, 12 peppercorns, 3 cardamom pods if available, a good pinch of dried marjoram, 1–2 teaspoons sugar, ½ teaspoon dill seeds, a few stalks of parsley and a bay leaf. Bring to the boil, then leave, covered, until cold. Strain before using, although you can add the seeds, pods and herbs to the jars.

APRICOT CHUTNEY

225 g/8 oz dried apricots
2 large onions, chopped
1 garlic clove, crushed
100 g/4 oz sultanas
350 g/12 oz demerara
sugar

2 tsp salt
450 ml/15 fl oz malt or
cider vinegar
juice of 1 lemon
1 tbls pickling spice

Cover the apricots with water and let them soak for a few hours, or overnight. Then drain them, keeping the liquid.

Chop the apricots roughly, then put them into a large saucepan with the onions, garlic, sultanas, sugar, salt, vinegar and lemon juice. Add the pickling spice, which can be tied in a piece of muslin if you wish – I leave them loose, as I like the crunchiness. Measure the reserved apricot liquid and if necessary make up to 300 ml/10 fl oz with water, and add that, too, to the pan. Bring to the boil, then let the mixture simmer gently, uncovered, for about 1 hour, or until it is thick and glossy.

While the chutney is cooking, prepare some special chutney jars by washing them well, then drying and sterilizing them in an oven preset to 140°C/275°F/Gas Mark ½, for 30 minutes. Spoon the chutney into the jars, cover with non-metal, vinegar-proof lids, and label.

MAKES ABOUT 1 KG/2 LB 2 OZ

OPPOSITE: *Mixed Vegetables in Oil*

CRANBERRY CONSERVE WITH PORT

To me, this glossy red conserve really smells and tastes of Christmas . . . It's good with puddings as well as savouries; try it spooned over ice cream or cheesecake; or with Greek yogurt.

225 g/8 oz cranberries
300 ml/10 fl oz water
450 g/1 lb granulated
  sugar

juice of 3 oranges
3 tbls port

I use horseradish jars to store Kumquats in Brandy if I don't have any mustard ones handy.

Wash the cranberries, then put them into a medium-large saucepan with the water and let them simmer gently until they are tender – about 4–5 minutes. Add the granulated sugar and orange juice, and heat gently until the sugar has dissolved, then let the mixture boil steadily until it reaches setting-point: 105°C/221°F on a sugar thermometer, or when a little of the liquid dropped on to a cold saucer wrinkles when you push it with your finger. Remove from the heat and stir in the port.

Pour the mixture into jars which have been warmed and sterilized by being baked in an oven preset to 140°C/275°F/Gas Mark ½, for 30 minutes.
MAKES ABOUT 1 KG/2 LB 2 OZ

CHEDDAR CHEESE AND BRANDY DIP

A good cheese dip, packed into an attractive container, such as a pretty pâté dish or even a special mug tied up with cellophane and ribbon, makes a thoughtful gift. This cheese dip is easy to make, tastes good, and keeps for several weeks.

100 g/4 oz Cheddar
  cheese, finely grated
25 g/1 oz soft butter

1 tbls brandy
freshly ground pepper

Put the cheese and butter into a bowl and beat together; gradually beat in the brandy and a small amount of water, if necessary, to make a creamy

consistency. Add a little pepper to taste.

Pack the mixture into your chosen container, cover, and refrigerate until needed.
MAKES ABOUT 175 G/6 OZ

KUMQUATS IN BRANDY

These tiny oranges, preserved in a brandy syrup, make an attractive gift – I generally add a handwritten label to the jar with a few ideas for using them. They're delicious spooned over thick yogurt, cream or ice cream; added to a fruit salad or, in small quantities, on their own or with a few whole, blanched almonds. You can eat them after a week, but they're much nicer if you can leave them for 4–6 weeks to mellow and mature.

375 g/12 oz kumquats
225 g/8 oz granulated
  sugar

3 tbls brandy

First choose a suitable jar or jars. This amount will fill one 600 ml/1 pint jar or two or three small ones, like old mustard jars. Wash the jars well, then dry and sterilize them by putting them into an oven set to 140°C/275°F/Gas Mark ½, for 30 minutes.

To prepare the kumquats, first wash them, then prick them all over with a darning needle or skewer. Put the sugar into a saucepan with 300 ml/10 fluid ounces of water and heat gently until the sugar has dissolved, then bring to the boil. Add the kumquats, cover and simmer for about 15 minutes, or until the kumquats are tender and shiny-looking.

Spoon the fruit into the sterilized jars, then add the brandy and enough of the cooking liquid to cover the kumquats. It's important to put plenty of fruit into the jar or jars, or the fruit will rise when you add the syrup. Screw on the lids. Store in a cool, dry place until required.
MAKES THREE 200 ML/6 FL OZ JARS

OPPOSITE: *Kumquats in Brandy*

CINNAMON SHORTBREADS

These cinnamon shortbreads are delicious with Chocolate Ice Cream (page 123) or Christmas Dried Fruit Salad (page 112), as well as being good on their own, with tea or coffee.

100 g/4 oz plain wholewheat flour
100 g/4 oz plain white flour
50 g/2 oz cornflour
50 g/2 oz semolina or ground rice

2–3 tsp powdered cinnamon
225 g/8 oz soft butter or vegan margarine
100 g/4 oz caster sugar

Set the oven to 170°C/325°F/Gas Mark 3 and grease a 19 cm × 29 cm/7½ inch × 11½ inch shallow tin with butter.

Sift the flours, semolina or ground rice and the cinnamon into a large bowl or food processor, adding the residue of bran from the sieve. Then put in the butter or margarine and the sugar. Whizz, or beat, all the ingredients together until they form a soft dough which leaves the sides of the bowl clean.

Press this into the tin, levelling the surface by pressing with the back of a metal spoon. Then prick the surface all over with a fork. Bake for about 45 minutes, until the shortbread is set and quite crispy on top and very lightly tinged with gold. It's more tricky to tell when these are done than with normal shortbreads because they are already rather brown! If you are in doubt, you can cut the shortbread and very carefully lift up one of the end pieces and look underneath it to see if it looks done underneath. If not, carefully put it back and let the shortbread cook for a bit longer. When it's done, cut it into sections, if you haven't already done so, and leave it to cool and crisp up in the tin.

This shortbread keeps well in a tin for several days, if it gets the chance, and also freezes well. It defrosts very quickly; you can use it almost straight from the freezer.
MAKES 24 SHORTBREADS

OPPOSITE: (left) Greek Shortbreads and (right) Cinnamon Shortbreads

GREEK SHORTBREADS

These are a cross between a sweet and a biscuit and make a lovely petit four, or, prettily packed, an attractive gift. Once they have been coated with rose water and icing sugar and then dried, they keep very well. I find the best place to buy rose water is from a Middle Eastern shop if there is one near to you – ask them which is the best. Otherwise some supermarkets and chemists have it; if you get it from the chemist, make sure it is suitable for cooking.

225 g/8 oz soft butter
50 g/2 oz caster sugar
1 egg yolk
275 g/10 oz plain flour
50 g/2 oz cornflour

95 g/3½ oz ground almonds
about 6 tbls triple-distilled rose water
375–450 g/12 oz–1 lb icing sugar

Set the oven to 170°C/325°F/Gas Mark 3 and line two large baking sheets with nonstick paper.

Put the butter and sugar into a bowl or food processor and whizz, or beat, them together until they are light, then beat in the egg yolk. Sift the flour and cornflour into the bowl, add the ground almonds, and mix gently until everything is combined.

Break off small pieces of the dough, about the size of a marble, and form them into crescents or barrel shapes. Put them on to the baking sheets, leaving a little space around them: they will expand a bit, but not too much. Bake for about 25 minutes, or until they are set but not coloured. Cool on a wire rack.

When the shortbreads are cool, put 6 tablespoons of rose water into a small bowl and sift the icing sugar into another bowl. Dip each shortbread quickly first into the rose water, then into the icing sugar. Return them to the wire rack and leave in a warm room for several hours. Pack them in a tin, or in boxes, sprinkling extra icing sugar between the layers, and on top.
MAKES ABOUT 70 SHORTBREADS

VEGAN VERSION
Just leave out the egg yolk, and use a vegan margarine instead of the butter.

MINI FLORENTINES

50 g/2 oz butter
50 g/2 oz caster sugar
50 g/2 oz glacé cherries,
 finely chopped
75 g/3 oz hazelnuts,
 finely chopped

25 g/1 oz mixed peel,
 finely chopped
2 tsp lemon juice
100 g/4 oz chocolate, use
 half plain and half white

Melt the butter in a saucepan, then add the sugar and bring to the boil, stirring all the time. Remove from the heat and stir in the cherries, hazelnuts, peel and lemon juice. Allow to cool slightly while you line two baking sheets with nonstick paper.

Set the oven to 180°C/350°F/Gas Mark 4.

Put little heaps of the mixture, about the size of a hazelnut, on the sheets, leaving room for them to spread. Bake for 5–6 minutes, until they are a light golden brown. Push the edges in with a knife to neaten, then leave them to cool on the paper.

Melt the chocolate in two separate bowls set over saucepans of simmering water, or in a microwave for 3–4 minutes, then spread over the smooth side of the florentines. Just before the chocolate sets, make wavy lines with a fork. Leave to cool completely.
MAKES ABOUT 60

MACAROONS

100 g/4 oz ground
 almonds
175 g/6 oz caster sugar
2 egg whites, lightly
 whisked

a few drops of almond
 essence
granulated sugar
12–14 almonds, blanched
 and halved

Set the oven to 180°C/350°F/Gas Mark 4 and line a baking sheet with nonstick paper.

Put the ground almonds into a bowl with the sugar and almond essence, then mix in enough of the egg white to make a stiff mixture. (You may not need all the egg white.) Either put teaspoonfuls of the mixture well apart on the baking sheet, or pipe small mounds, using a piping bag with a 1 cm/½ inch plain nozzle, allowing room to spread. Sprinkle with sugar and top with half an almond.

Bake for 15–20 minutes, or until set and golden brown. Allow to firm up on the paper, then lift off on to a wire rack to finish cooling.
MAKES 12–14 MACAROONS

SHAPED BISCUITS

150 g/6 oz butter or
 vegan margarine
50 g/2 oz icing sugar
100 g/4 oz plain white
 flour

100 g/4 oz wholewheat
 flour
glacé icing, sweets,
 hundreds and thousands,
 melted chocolate, etc., to
 decorate

Set the oven to 180°C/350°F/Gas Mark 4 and line two large baking sheets with nonstick paper.

Put the butter or margarine into a bowl with the icing sugar and beat together until they are light and creamy. Add the flours and beat again to make a dough. You can add flavourings at this point: some grated lemon rind, cinnamon, ginger or a drop or two of real vanilla essence are good. On a lightly floured board, roll out the dough to 2.5 mm/⅛ inch, then cut into all kinds of Chrismassy shapes – stars, angels, Christmas trees, and so on. Put the biscuits on the baking sheets – they won't spread much.

Bake for about 10 minutes, or until the biscuits look golden brown, set and are browning a little more at the edges. Leave to cool on the sheets, then decorate, using glacé icing, little sweets, hundreds and thousands, some melted chocolate, to make them look really colourful. The children will probably love to help with this. If you're planning to hang them on the tree, punch a hole on an outside edge before baking so that you can thread them later.
MAKES 18–20 BISCUITS

OPPOSITE: *Mini Florentines, made with light and dark chocolate*

SNOWFLAKES

The children will love to help with all of these biscuits - baking them and hanging them on the tree afterwards.

2 egg whites
100 g/4 oz caster sugar
15 g/½ oz finely chopped
  skinned hazelnuts
15 g/½ oz preserving
  sugar

Set the oven to 150°C/300°F/Gas Mark 2 and line two large baking sheets with nonstick paper.

Whisk the egg whites until stiff, as for meringues, then whisk in the caster sugar. Put the mixture into a piping bag fitted with a shell nozzle – about 5 mm/¼ inch across. Pipe blobs of meringue on to the baking sheets in the form of snowflakes – with six points. Don't make them too high as they will rise a bit.

Mix together the nuts and preserving sugar and sprinkle these over the top of the snowflakes. Bake for about 1 hour, until they have dried out and are crisp. Leave to cool on the sheets.

These are extremely popular with children and look very pretty on the tree. Make a little hole in the middle of your snowflake before baking so that you can thread them.

STAINED GLASS WINDOW BISCUITS

75 g/3 oz plain white
  flour
75 g/3 oz wholewheat
  flour
100 g/4 oz butter or
  vegan margarine
40 g/1½ oz icing sugar
about 24 boiled sweets of
  different colours: red,
  orange, green, yellow and
  purple

Set the oven to 180°C/350°F/Gas Mark 4 and line two large baking sheets with nonstick paper.

Beat together the flours, butter or margarine and icing sugar, to make a dough. On a lightly floured board, roll out the dough to a depth of 2.5 mm/⅛ inch. Cut out shapes which are large enough to take a boiled sweet in the centre, allowing for the sweet to spread a bit. Then cut a circle out of the middle of the biscuits, about the size that the sweet will spread to. I use the round end of a piping nozzle for this. Put the biscuits on the baking sheets – they won't spread much – and pop a boiled sweet into each centre.

Bake for about 10 minutes, or until the sweets have melted and the biscuits look golden brown, set and are browning a little more at the edges. Leave to cool on the sheets, but before they get completely firm, make a little hole in the top of each, well away from the edges, through which you can thread some cord to hang them on the tree.
MAKES ABOUT 24 BISCUITS

GINGER BEARS

50 g/2 oz butter
25 g/1 oz caster sugar
50 g/2 oz white flour
50 g/2 oz wholewheat
  flour
1 tsp baking powder
1 tsp ground ginger
1 tbls golden syrup
sweets, melted chocolate,
  etc, to decorate

Set the oven to 180°C/350°F/Gas Mark 4 and line two large baking sheets with nonstick paper.

Put the butter or margarine into a bowl with the caster sugar and beat together until they are light and creamy. Add the flours, baking powder, ginger and syrup, and beat again to make a dough. On a lightly floured board, roll out the dough to 2.5 mm/⅛ inch, then cut into teddy bears. Put the biscuits on the baking sheets – they won't spread much.

Bake for about 10 minutes, or until the biscuits look golden brown, set and are browning a little more at the edges. Leave to cool on the sheets, then decorate, using glacé icing, little sweets, hundreds and thousands, some melted chocolate.
MAKES ABOUT 10–12 BEARS

OPPOSITE: *A selection of Christmas tree biscuits: Snowflakes, Stained Glass Window Biscuits, Ginger Bears and Shaped Biscuits, page 148*

MARZIPAN SWEETS

These are fun to make with children – like play dough, but more satisfactory because you can eat the results! Although you can use home-made almond paste, I find bought white almond paste/marzipan is better because it is less likely to get oily when rolled and moulded.

To colour the marzipan, take a small amount of marzipan, roll it into a ball, then break it open and put a few drops of colouring in the centre. Knead it until it is evenly coloured. When the fruits have dried a little you can paint on extra details if you wish. Put a little cake colouring on a piece of greaseproof paper, dip a clean, fine paint brush into this and paint the models as required.

To make Santa's sack, colour a piece of marzipan brown, flatten it, then gather up the edges to make a sack. Fill this with 'presents' made from pieces of coloured marzipan – squares, rectangles and other shapes – with bows and cords made of small pieces of marzipan. If you feel up to it, you can make a yellow teddy bear (or other appealing toy!) to stick out of the top of the sack. Use a cylinder of yellow marzipan for the body, a ball on top for the head (pulled out to a point for the nose) and stick on little ears and long 'sausages' to make arms and legs. Some red and green crackers look nice as part of the display, too: for these, use cylinders of marzipan, indented to make the part you pull, and fringed with a cocktail stick. Leaves of holly can be cut from green marzipan with a holly cutter, and decorated with a few red marzipan berries.

To make Marzipan Fruits, roll out balls of orange marzipan to make oranges, running them over a fine grater to get an orange-peel texture: finish with a clove stuck in the end to make the stalk. Make apples and pears by shaping light greeny yellow marzipan and sticking the pointed end of cloves into the tops to make stems. The apples can be painted with a flush of red when they have dried a bit. For bananas, roll out 'sausages' of yellow marzipan, then curve them round and join several together to make a bunch. These can be painted with some flecks of brown (cake colouring or cocoa mixed with a little water) when they have set a bit. Grapes are made from purple marzipan, rolled into tiny balls and stuck together to make a bunch.

OPPOSITE: *Marzipan Sweets*

VEGAN FUDGE

The secrets of making good fudge, vegan or otherwise, are to use a really large saucepan and not to try to make too much fudge at once; and to use a sugar thermometer, which takes all the guesswork out of it. This is a basic vegan fudge which you can flavour in different ways. For a chocolate version, beat in 100 g/ 4 oz plain chocolate, broken up, when you take the fudge off the heat and start beating it.

700 g/1½ lb caster sugar	2 tsp vanilla essence
600 ml/1 pint soya milk	100 g/4 oz walnut pieces
100 g/4 oz vegan	(optional)
margarine	

First line an 18 cm/7 inch square tin with nonstick paper.

Put the sugar, soya milk and margarine into a large, heavy-based saucepan and heat gently until the margarine has melted and the sugar dissolved. Bring to the boil and let it simmer steadily until the temperature reaches 120°C/240°F on a sugar thermometer, or a small piece dropped into a cup of cold water forms a soft ball. Remove from the heat immediately and add the vanilla essence and walnuts if you are using them, then cool it quickly by placing it in a bowl of cold water.

Beat the mixture for a few minutes, until it thickens and is on the point of setting, then pour it into the prepared tin and leave to set.

When the fudge is firm, cut it into squares using a sharp knife.

MAKES ABOUT 40 SQUARES

COCONUT ICE

This is a tradional recipe for pink-and-white stripy coconut ice, and it's vegan. It's particularly easy to make if you have a sugar thermometer.

450 g/1 lb granulated	100 g/4 oz desiccated
sugar	coconut
150 ml/5 fl oz water	red vegetable colouring
1 tsp vanilla essence	

First line an 18 cm/7 inch square tin with nonstick paper.

Put the granulated sugar and water into a medium-sized, heavy-based saucepan and heat gently, without boiling, until the sugar has dissolved. Bring to the boil and let it simmer steadily until the temperature reaches 120°C/240°F on a sugar thermometer, or a little of the syrup dropped into a cup of cold water forms a soft ball. Remove from the heat immediately and add the vanilla essence and desiccated coconut.

Stir the mixture for 5–10 minutes, or until it begins to thicken and set, then pour half of it into the prepared tin and smooth it level. Colour the remaining half pale pink with a drop or two of colouring, then pour this on top of the white coconut ice, spreading it to the edges and making sure it's level. Press it all down quite firmly with the back of a spoon, and leave it to harden.

Turn the coconut ice out and cut it into squares using a sharp knife.

MAKES ABOUT 700 G/1½ LB

CHRISTMAS WRAPPING

It's always a pleasure to receive a present which has been attractively wrapped, and you do not need to be particularly artistic in order to achieve a very pretty result. Simple shapes are easiest to wrap, so it can be helpful to put the gift into a box first; or make a virtue out of an odd shape by turning it into a cracker or a Christmas bauble. In the case of a bottle, don't even try to conceal it, but just wrap it luxuriously, with an outer layer of cellophane and lots of ribbons, or an extension of the wrapping paper cut into a fringe . . . Stick to one or two colours – plain is always safer than patterned or, if you use patterned paper, pick up one of the colours with a ribbon or bow; or you can use gold or silver ribbon, which always looks good.

Bauble

Crackers

Bottle with outer layer of cellophane over coloured paper

Bottle with wrapping paper cut into a fringe

Curling ends of ribbon with scissors

155